THE 5000
AND THE POWER TANGLE

BY THE SAME AUTHOR
New Law and Practice of Parish Administration
(Longcross Press)

THE 5000
AND THE POWER TANGLE

Charles Arnold-Baker

JOHN MURRAY

To
A. W. B.

'But is there not a certain tribe of infidels called Ingliz?' said I, 'the most unaccountable people on earth who live in an island and make pen-knives?'

JAMES MORIER: *Hajji Baba of Ispahan*

CONTENTS

CONTENTS

PART FOUR: EXTERNAL AFFAIRS

ix

CONTENTS

PART FIVE:
RECAPITULATION AND CONCLUSION

PART SIX: APPENDICES

DIAGRAMS, CHARTS AND MAPS

PREFACE

The excuse for writing this work is that only a tiny minority of people have any idea how the country is governed and very few ever have much time to find out. This book is therefore intentionally short. It is a description, not a work of reference, and suffers from all the defects of compression, superficiality and arbitrary selection of material; the serious student is strongly advised to read *Erskine May*, Cross, Jennings and other masters of the subject (*see* Short list of Books on p. 176).

Much of this book is derived from personal experience and consists of material which has at one time or another been necessary to the author in his other work. Some of it, of course, is second-hand: a good deal is not. For the reader this must carry a warning; he must be careful not to be led too far by a personal point of view.

The outline description offered here is that of modern working institutions and in order to avoid blurring the picture many matters of interest or importance have been either omitted altogether or relegated to the maps, diagrams, the list of events or the glossary.

The author owes many debts of gratitude in connection with this book: especially to his wife and to Mrs Janet Young of Wychwood School, Oxford, for their amiable criticism and wisdom, to Reproduction Drawings Ltd for interpreting my visual aids, and not least to Miss Ann Rowen who typed a tiresome manuscript.

London and Gibraltar   C. A-B.
    1966

INTRODUCTION

At the centre of every human society there is a small group of people who, between them, manage it and whose decisions can affect the future of the rest. This group has never, anywhere, yet been wholly able to impose its collective will because even if it needs only a minimum of armed retainers it still has to contend with human inertia and stupidity, natural hazards, and the consequences of its own mistakes.

The difference between a tyrannical and a constitutional state lies primarily in two factors. Under a tyranny such as the Napoleonic Empire or Communist Russia the ruling group is minute and self-appointing; in a constitutional State it is slightly larger and its members are drawn from a variety of sources. This contrast between the monolithic and the diverse is felt in all walks of life: fanaticism is contrasted with compromise, an accepted artistic convention with a variety of schools, a national purpose with something more free and easy, dullness with entertainment. Life in democratic Athens may have been miserable for some but it was seldom boring; in regimented Sparta they ordered things differently. Moreover it is only in a tyrannical State that the ruling group can be said to have a collective will: in a larger, constitutional group there is always opposition and compromise.

When a monolithic and very small ruling group begins to increase and diversify, the nation is moving away from tyranny and similarly the contraction and simplification of such a group means that it is moving towards it.

The United Kingdom has been and still is a constitutional State with a ruling group which I have called 'The 5000', partly because its number is something of that order and partly because, for reasons which will appear, it is necessary to use a neutral term. The British Constitution consists of The 5000, the rules and habits by which they conduct their business with each other, especially the factors determining the speed at which they work and the instruments which they employ. The rules and habits take up most of this short book because they concern issues of great range and variety. Any substantial change in any of these major features is a constitutional amendment, and as it happens some such changes can be made by processes so informal that the public never hears of them at all. It is time that more attention were paid to them. I study this in more detail in Part Three of this book. The reader may complain that he does not find enough about The 5000 themselves in these pages. It is a valid criticism, but it is quite remarkably difficult to focus exactly on any definite number of people who hold power at any time: they change so quickly. The number has been chosen to give a broad indication of the scale on which our search should lie.

It may at first seem surprising that in a nation of 56 millions it should be possible to speak of so small a number as 5000. It can be argued that to this limited figure there should be added, say, the body of associates who push them into prominence, or even so large a body as the whole of the floating vote. This is of course a tenable view, but I do not think that it adequately isolates those who make or directly influence decisions of state. There is a difference between a king and a kingmaker. The answer is that ruling groups must be small to be any use and that in many countries they are or have been (relative to the population) much smaller. In 18th-century Poland the ruling group became so large that the State was reduced to anarchy and eventual partition. France under Louis XIV had about 18 million people: they were ruled by the King, his family, a few familiars, some churchmen and soldiers and one or two ministers numbering with high officials and the genuinely influential probably less than one hundred in all.

Part One

OUTLINE OF THE SYSTEM

1

GEOGRAPHY

The United Kingdom of Great Britain and Northern Ireland with its dependencies consists of seven distinct parts, namely, England, Wales, Scotland, Northern Ireland, the Isle of Man, Jersey and Guernsey with Alderney and Sark.

These divisions have arisen by historical accident; they continue for different reasons and purposes and exhibit strikingly divergent traits. Thus English is now the universal language but three others (Welsh, Gaelic and French) are traditional while others such as Polish have been recently imported. England (except Monmouthshire) has an established episcopal church which extends to the Channel Islands and Man; in Scotland there is also an established church, but it is Presbyterian; neither Wales (with Monmouth) nor Northern Ireland has an established church at all. There are three systems of law, namely, English Law which with growing variations obtains in Wales, Man and Northern Ireland; the Civil Law of Scotland, and the Norman French Custom of the Channel Islands; as might be expected these are administered by judicial organizations peculiar to themselves and so, though England and Wales have one network of courts in common, the other five countries have legal institutions which are entirely different from the English and each other's; in each case, however, the final court of appeal is in London.

Other institutions also reflect the divergent climates, histories and habits of these ancient divisions. Of these perhaps the most noticeable, if not necessarily the most important, are the patterns established for education and for local government; these are nearly the same in England and Wales but alter progressively further from the 'English' standard as we reach Scotland, visit Ulster or take ship for Man or the Channel Islands.

This regional diversity, again, is strongly expressed in the nature of the great central organizations by which the components are governed. The Sovereign in Parliament can, and with varying frequency does enact laws for all the seven territories, and there is no doubt that they are supreme in all seven, but the detailed position is more complex. Neither Man nor the Channel Isles are represented in Parliament and each has a Lieutenant Governor representing the Crown and an ancient legislature (called 'Tynwald' in the Isle of Man and 'The States' in the other two) of its own. Ulster has a governor and Parliament together with a cluster of locally responsible ministries, and in addition, it is represented in the House of Commons at Westminster; England, Scotland and Wales on the other hand elect the bulk of this House and, in addition, Scotland is specially represented in the House of Lords by the remnants of its own peerage, but none of them has separate parliaments. Finally, the Ministers of the London Government are responsible to the London Parliament in some cases (such as foreign affairs) for all seven territories; in others only for some of them; Scotland has a Secretary of State with a department in Edinburgh which is a miniature government reflecting most of the internal departments at Whitehall, and Wales also has a Secretary of State who has a somewhat incomplete office at Cardiff.

There are, moreover, further complicating factors arising out of the special position of the United Kingdom in the Commonwealth. The Sovereign, as Head of the Commonwealth, is the living symbol of a certain similarity of outlook shared by its numerous and distant States; in addition, the Sovereign reigns as monarch in some of them such as Canada and New Zealand. The Crown has consequently an unique international status whose character is unavoidably influenced by the fact that its wearer ordinarily resides in England. Moreover, the United Kingdom is responsible in various ways for colonial territories such as Gibraltar and for protectorates like the Kingdom of Tonga. The Privy Council acts as a final court of appeal for some of the dominions and all the colonies: it administers over a dozen entirely different systems of law and was till recently the only genuine international court of justice in the world. The Westminster Parliament can legislate even for some of the independent States if they so request (as frequently happened in the case of Canada) and citizens of commonwealth countries and of the Irish Republic are eligible to become voters in United Kingdom elections.

The Rhodesian unilateral declaration of independence (or rebellion) of 1965 created some curious constitutional problems. The policy of the British Government was attacked by other members of the Commonwealth, some of whom withdrew their High Commissioners from London and left their interests to be protected by some other Commonwealth government. Some denounced Britain in the United Nations and sought help from foreign powers against British policy. In 1966 the British Government invited the United Nations to help to put down the rebellion by imposing compulsory sanctions and to this the Security Council agreed. Thus the moral cohesion of the Commonwealth was severely damaged and a theoretically domestic dispute was deliberately dragged into an international forum.

5

2

ORIGINS

East of the Pennines Anglo-Saxon England originally stretched from Edinburgh to the Channel, but on the west only from the Ribble to the Tamar and it omitted Wales. The Normans began by devastating the north so that except in Durham there was thereafter no effective government north of a line from the Humber to Southport. This weakness eventually enabled the Scots to establish their eastern border down to Berwick where it remains. Farther south central rule was imposed or reimposed in three distinct stages: conquest, colonization and assimilation. Cornwall was pacified first but retains to this day a special position as a duchy vested in the monarch's eldest son. Lancashire was not organized until the 13th Century; the English county system was introduced into about half of Wales in the 13th Century, but the rest was under colonial military rule by Lords Marcher until Tudor times. This Marcher system also existed on the Scottish frontier which was eventually moved on the west to its present position on the Solway Firth.

The Saxons were ruled by kings who took advice from those most readily available; these latter were their friends and, which was often the same thing, their household officials, together with their principal military officers, and after the organization of Christianity, the bishops. Amongst these councillors, territorial magnates made their appearance very early – because it would have been impolitic to ignore them. Subject to the restraints of custom, the decisions were in theory made by the King with or without the advice of his councillors. Actually the situation differed from reign to reign and even within reigns. Strong kings made their own decisions: weak ones had decisions

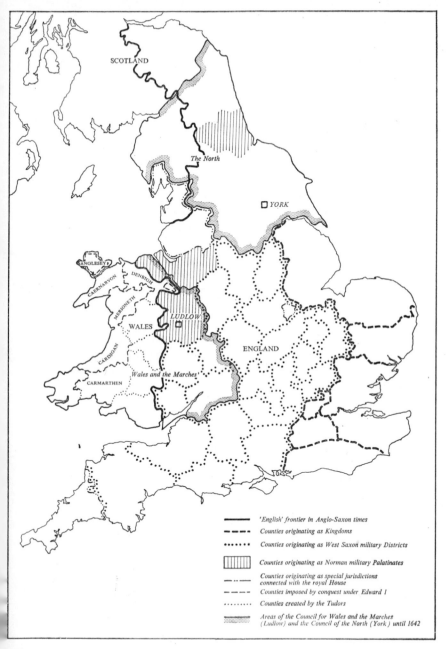

SCOTLAND

The North

☐ YORK

ANGLESEY

CAERNARVON
DENBIGH
MERIONETH

WALES

LUDLOW ☐

ENGLAND

CARDIGAN

Wales and the Marches

CARMARTHEN

———	'English' frontier in Anglo-Saxon times
– – –	Counties originating as Kingdoms
••••••	Counties originating as West Saxon military Districts
‖‖‖‖	Counties originating as Norman military *Palatinates*
–·–·–	Counties originating as special jurisdictions connected with the royal House
– – – –	Counties imposed by conquest under Edward I
········	Counties created by the Tudors
░░░░░	Areas of the Council for Wales and the Marches (Ludlow) and the Council of the North (York) until 1642

Fig. 1. HISTORICAL GEOGRAPHY

made for them and sometimes no doubt absence or illness placed real power in the hands of deputies. Physically the West Saxon kings from whom the present royal house is descended were not robust.

The 11th Century saw the introduction of feudal notions. It is not necessary to decide the disputed issue whether the Normans brought feudalism or came to it; the important point is that it imposed upon the King an obligation to hold a court which had to be consulted on grave issues and gave to the territorial magnates the right to attend it. This court of great men is the ancestor of the House of Lords and by a fortunate coincidence the Church, which was the only large organized body of educated people, was heavily represented because the ecclesiastical magnates had great territorial possessions. The lay lords were in a minority until the 16th Century even though they had most of the real power, but because literacy was an ecclesiastical virtue the King's officials were mostly churchmen. The court was full of administrators.

The monarchs of the early Middle Ages drew their resources from three main springs: there were the vast royal estates, the feudal services of their tenants and certain taxes and dues of decreasing value of which the most important was the Danegeld. By the early 13th Century these were becoming inadequate, especially if it became necessary to wage a war. In fact foreign wars could only be carried on if they were successful, but as a matter of fact the monarchs at this period suffered defeats. It was King John who lost Normandy.* The royal income had not kept pace with costs: if funds had to be obtained it became necessary to ask – not command – the great men to concede the necessary amounts; and they, of course, demanded a growing right to interfere in the way their money was spent.

But 'their' money came from tenants and trading communities with independent rights, and thus it was difficult – sometimes impossible – to collect taxes from this lower population

* Except for the Channel Isles, whose law is founded on the Custom of Rouen at the date (1207) of the evacuation of the Duchy.

without the reluctant help of the lords, who were held responsible by those below them for unpopular measures in the same sort of way as they themselves blamed the King. The 13th Century was a time when this question of government, government finance and tax collection was a matter of sanguinary dispute. It led to the first of the constitutional civil wars, and by the end of it there had emerged an institution which we have today, namely, a parliament of two Houses. If the feudal King's Court was the ancestor of the House of Lords, the refusal of the lords to answer in taxation matters for their sub-tenants was the prime motive of the Kings in calling together a body which represented those tenants and the towns. In the House of Commons the borough members were from the beginning in a large majority, but it was the country minority which for centuries held the leadership. Indeed the town members were often terrified of their duties and in one case members fled on hearing of their election, and had to be taken to Parliament by force.

In these early days the function of the Commons was to assent to the decisions made by their betters. They were only taken seriously when the lords were unwilling to concede something (usually money) to the Crown but could find no good argument for their refusal. In only one pre-Tudor Parliament did the Commons take an independent line and even then they took the precaution (usual in the Middle Ages) of inviting two lords to sit with them. This was the Parliament associated with Wat Tyler's insurrection and the attempt was a failure.

Looking back, the important feature of the Middle Ages was that Parliament met with regularity so that the nation became accustomed to it and it developed procedures, habits and rights. These parliaments were doubtless bullied, bribed or packed but the point was reached where the form of the institution was settled and its legal supremacy assumed. The political struggles of the 15th Century (the so called Wars of the Roses) were, of course, largely in military form, but when occasional resort was made to legalism it was a parliament constituted in accordance with established custom that was called to give due form to a situation imposed by force. It did not occur to anyone to try and transfer the supremacy to some other institution. In a journal left by the secretary of a Czech nobleman who visited England in the latter half of the 15th Century there is a description of Parliament and its procedure: it is not very different now.

The Tudors were faced with a difficult situation from which Parliament offered them their only real chance of escape. Their title to the Crown was slight; the recent civil wars had destroyed much of the nobility and inflicted serious damage in other ways. Parliament had become an institution which stood for stability so that it was natural and politic for them to identify themselves with it. They governed with a ruthless hand but they governed through Parliament; all their great revolutionary measures were taken with its assent and in the form of legislation, but to this they added something of their own. The technique of the three great Tudors was to kick their subjects in the direction in which they really wanted to go and their century-long administration produced four major constitutional developments.

The dissolution of the monasteries changed the balance of the government. It drastically reduced the number of churchmen available for administrative tasks at the centre; it abolished the ecclesiastical majority in the House of Lords by ending the rights of the mitred abbots; and it created a powerful class of country gentry based upon the spoils of the monasteries to whom most of the functions of county administration were committed. It also compelled the government to take an interest in social welfare which hitherto had been the accepted concern of ecclesiastical, especially monastic charity. The deathbed of the monasteries was the cradle of local government. Lastly as a corollary there came into existence a powerful policy-making instrument – the Privy Council – which was able to enforce its will through a specially expeditious court (the Star Chamber) and by means of regional machinery in the form of the Council of the North at York and the Council of Wales and the Marches sitting at Ludlow. At the same time Wales was incorporated into England, the Marcher Lordships were abolished and the county system extended to the whole country. The standardization of civil government in the new areas required special measures and the councils at York and Ludlow lasted as local watchdogs for Westminster until the Civil War.

The arrival of the Stuarts unified the Crowns of England and Scotland, and though the two countries were to have separate parliaments, governments and even currency for a century, the two nations acquired a common allegiance. Moreover, the process of accretion to the English central nucleus, which had brought Welshmen into government positions under the Tudors, brought Scotsmen into important positions under the Stuarts. The most important feature of the situation was, however, the fact that protestantism (of two different sorts) became the ruling religious sentiment in the whole island; all forms of protestantism originate in revolt, and religion now sanctioned the sturdy local independence of the gentry whose fortunes had been made out of the monasteries. It had also a further consequence of incalculable importance: ever since the 13th Century Ireland had been in a turmoil caused by civil war and partially successful efforts at conquest by the English. The Irish mostly remained Roman Catholic so that religion became a strong element in Irish national feelings; in the north, however, a series of successful English and Scots colonizations took place so that much of the land, capital and enterprise of Ulster was in the hands of protestants whose loyalties were this side of the Irish Sea.

The Stuart epoch was one of profound and violent political conflict. At the beginning the two great issues were the control of taxation and of the army, and these were decided in two civil wars in which Charles I was defeated. It is an oversimplification to treat this conflict as a direct collision between Crown and Parliament: if a majority of the members of the Houses fought against Charles a large minority were on his side, and his defeat and execution brought not parliamentary supremacy but the suppression of parliamentary government by the soldiers.

In a religious age few could long support those who had laid violent hands on the Lord's Anointed and it was not to establish a military despotism that either side had fought a war. After Oliver Cromwell's death the country turned with revulsion and relief to a parliamentary monarchy in which the King ruled by divine right but Parliament prevented him from ruling too much. The division of power was not exact or well defined so that there were further controversies conducted by Charles II comparatively peacefully and by James II with a show of force. In a second revolution the latter was driven into exile and his sister Mary II together with her husband William III were brought to the throne on the condition that they should accept the Bill of Rights of 1689. This codified those liberties against the government which were then thought important; the Crown was forbidden to levy taxes or maintain a standing army in peacetime without parliamentary consent and the independence of the common law was henceforth guaranteed against the Crown by making it impossible to dismiss the judges.

The French wars under Dutch William and Anne brought important changes. The Stuart Pretender represented a Scottish dynasty and lived at the headquarters of the enemy: military necessity, therefore, brought about the unification of England and Scotland under a single parliament and government. The Act of Union of 1707 did not, however, assimilate their other institutions and much of Scotland remained under the heritable jurisdictions of clan chieftains until the rebellion of 1745.

A later consequence of the French wars was the demonstration that the Commons had become the predominating force at Westminster. The rise of the House had been in progress for a century and its power was now confirmed because it alone could back the war with the necessary money. The government which in 1712 decided to abandon its allies and the Duke of Marlborough's policies was able with Commons support to do so in the teeth of the House of Lords.

12

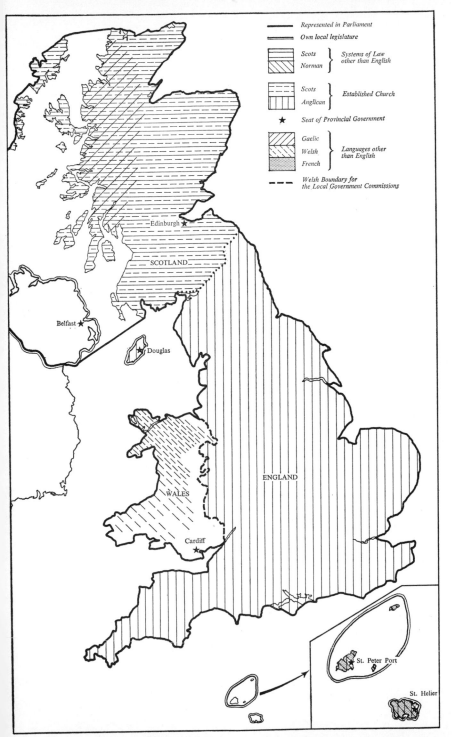

Fig. 2. NATIONAL DIFFERENCES

The 17th Century was the time of the rise of a politically conscious class consisting mainly of the country gentry and the merchants and financiers of the larger towns. With it was born the political party. The Civil War was fought about issues of principle on which men differed in an organized, if violent manner. The Restoration put an end to civil war as a means of settling disputes, and the subsequent division of powers between Crown and Parliament both encouraged and distorted the habit of organization for political ends. If Parliament was to be the ultimate arbiter of policy then opposed opinions would naturally be organized within it as parties, but since leadership of policy was still accepted as residing in the Crown, the Sovereign played a part resembling that of a party leader. Opposition was initially dangerous because the distinction between treason to the Monarch and opposition to his policies was not at first clear, and indeed in the last forty years of the century several politicians suffered punishment for acts which would now be regarded as merely political. Politics was still a dangerous trade especially if the Sovereign happened, as he sometimes did, to change his mind.

One consequence of this was that politicians not merely protected themselves as far as they could against the operations of the law, but – the Civil War being well within recollection – sought to entrench themselves so that their enemies would find it dangerous to move the law at all. They started, in fact, to bid for public support. The electors were few in number but they had to vote openly, and could be influenced by the opinion or the rotten eggs of the rest. The birth of parties and of newspapers coincided, but it was no coincidence, and the party managers of those days rapidly developed highly effective public relations techniques. The modern mass party was on its way.

Leaving aside the fascinating details of party history the English system has certain characteristics which have shown astounding endurance. The electoral system has always favoured two parties as against a third or fourth, so that new men with new opinions have generally sought to influence events through the two major existing organizations. In so doing their ideas have undergone a certain dilution and the parties have themselves received a certain admixture. Both have consequently shown a tendency to expel or reject extremists, and to move with the times.

The distinction between the two parties has always been one rather of outlook and temperament than of hard and fast doctrine or policy. The Conservative or Tory Party has never opposed change for its own sake and has seldom deliberately set out to undo the work of a reformist government; it is in fact a well-known jibe at the Tories that they manage cheerfully to administer any reform which they have inherited and that since they opposed the passage of the reform they must be devoid of principle. On the other side the reformist parties have had a more chequered history and a variety of names: this is understandable because any reform must be aimed at an objective and when that has been attained a new objective of, perhaps, an entirely different character appears. The Whigs of the 18th Century were succeeded by the Liberals in the 19th and they in the 20th by Labour.

In the 18th Century interest shifts to the development of a more modern administrative machine. Habit dies hard; the development tended to take the form of a struggle between Crown and Parliament because this was the form of controversy with which men were familiar. The Crown admittedly depended on Parliament for troops and taxes, but administration was still based upon the medieval principle that an office holder was paid out of revenues attached, like property, to his office. The holder, for instance, of a certain clerkship would always be entitled to a fixed fee whenever an Exchequer tally was issued even though he had no knowledge of it and had taken no part in the procedure. Most offices were in the gift of the Crown and they were very numerous. Their incomes varied from the fabulous to the trivial and so could be made to suit any situation: they formed a great source of influence for anyone who had the confidence of the King, and offers of jobs ('jobbery') were used with growing success to procure support in Parliament for policies.

But since the death of Anne, the King was a German who spoke no English, and the Privy Council which had always met in the Sovereign's presence now ceased for lack of comprehension to discuss important questions and became increasingly formal. Policy fell into the hands of the 'Cabinet', that is to say the more influential ministers headed by the Minister upon whom the King was most apt to rely. The control of money was the lynchpin of the system and this Minister usually held – and now always holds – the headship of the Treasury. Unofficially but universally he was called the Prime Minister, though this title only received statutory recognition as late as 1935.

If the Prime Minister had fair parliamentary support and the royal confidence, the power of Crown patronage could be used to influence the influential in the interests of his policy and to make his fortune and that of his friends. On the other hand, if the Minister and the King fell out the power could be and was used against him. This might have been tolerable if the country had remained poor, sparsely populated and unimportant, but it did not: the 18th Century was the first great time of commercial, naval and colonial expansion, of industrial invention and agricultural improvement. The population began to increase, to diversify and to migrate. The medieval framework of administration no longer fitted the facts and the administrative situation was far too complicated and the problems too big for posts in the public service to be used as counters in political intrigues. The last decades of the century saw the beginning of the end of this dispensation: the wholesale abolition of sinecures cleared the way for the introduction of rational methods and sensibly, if incidentally, diminished the power of the Crown.

The forces which drove governments into administrative reform also made the ancient Parliament out of date. Many places represented in the Commons since the 14th Century had ceased to be significant – or even, like Old Sarum, to exist – while great towns such as Manchester had grown up without representation of any sort. Many seats in the Commons were controlled through bribery or pressure, and the controllers' interest could be purchased. Patronage was as much a characteristic of Parliament as of the Crown. If it often brought superbly able men such as Pitt, Fox and Wellington to the fore it also prevented Parliament from effectively representing and acting as the safety valve of the nation. In the thirty years after Waterloo England was on the verge of social revolution; legally the nature of Parliament could be changed only by a bill passed by itself. Its unwillingness to do so provoked agitation, outrage and bloodshed. Most of Bristol had to be burned down before the great Reform Bill was passed in 1832.

The principle then established was that the Commons should be elected by voters whose qualifications in given circumstances would always be the same. The franchise was at first very restricted but was gradually widened, so that by 1914 it included almost all adult males – but not a single woman.

Meanwhile administrative reform at all levels became a major preoccupation. The chartered corporations of the towns were reformed in 1834 and the foundations of the modern examination-recruited civil service laid thirty years later. The population had multiplied and there had been a wild rush into the urban centres where people lived in insanitary squalor. Disease forced local reform on governments; a beginning was made with sewers. The modern urban (1875) and rural (1894) district councils started life as public health authorities with drains as their first care. The widening of the franchise and the growth of the councils brought a change in county administration in 1888: county councils then took over the functions which the justices had exercised since Tudor times.

The growth of the industrial classes had changed the character of the House of Commons; the Lords remained a hereditary assembly based not on industry but on land. As usual the next difficulty arose on a matter of money; in the political clash

17

just before the First World War the legal power of the Lords was reduced. By the Parliament Act of 1911 its (seldom used) control of money bills was abolished and its ability to stop other public legislation reduced to a power of delay. The Commons thus became in theory the dominant partner in Parliament.

This domination was not, however, a triumph. Other facts supervened to undermine it. The creation of mass electorates made it increasingly necessary for candidates to rely upon party organizations to get themselves elected. Once in Parliament they were under the pressure of the controllers of such organizations to toe the party line in order to get themselves re-elected. As a protection against Irish filibustering, governments had introduced the timetable motions and these became instruments for steam-rollering government measures through the Commons after 1921 and despite the disappearance of the Irish members. The power of party machines increased with each increase in the electorate: the complete enfranchisement of women between the wars doubled it and so the cornerstone of the power of the Commons – the real as opposed to the legal control of money – began to crack. The liberty of the individual member to vote as he pleased and even to say what he pleased was restricted seriously if not absolutely by an unbending party discipline which has shifted the effective power in the State away from Parliament to a combination of senior politicians in the cabinet and senior civil servants.

The earliest signs of this appeared innocently and significantly only two years after the Parliament Act, when the collection of taxes for a short period in each year on the authority of a resolution of the Commons alone was legalized; the constitutional significance of this has often been overlooked. The annual budget is prepared in the deepest secrecy and its contents are divulged suddenly for the purpose of obtaining the necessary resolutions: thus the administrative machine and the taxpayers are committed to a year's fiscal policy at the shortest imaginable notice. In theory the resolutions can be rescinded: in practice the consequences of backing out of the commitments involved and the difficulty of repaying taxes already collected would be so far-reaching and destructive that this will never happen. Thus it is a peculiar feature of the British Constitution that the most important regular event of the year is prepared outside Parliament and rushed through it at such speed and with so little notice that its consequences are never properly considered by ordinary members.

The detailed control of money has also tended to slip away from the Commons. It was necessary to keep secret the appropriations required for the First World War. Afterwards the sums raised and spent by the government and the fields of such expenditure had become so vast that it was difficult for the individual member to follow exactly what was going on. In the Second World War secrecy on warlike appropriations was total and again after it government action was extended to new fields such as the health and welfare services, and to the regulation of the economy through the budget and the control of borrowing and rates of interest. In the management of these matters the government has at its beck and call the civil service and its research organization: though the creation of a Parliamentary Commissioner or Ombudsman may go some way towards filling the gap, the House of Commons has no equivalent body. The individual members even when not harassed by the party organizations are at a disadvantage through the sheer difficulty of discovering the facts. Nowadays the House habitually passes large overspending of the budget by way of supplementary estimate without significant debate: in the ten years between 1953 and 1962 over 2,000 million pounds was authorized in this way; and in 1952 the Inland Revenue was empowered to take security for payment from persons who might be liable for a tax under a Commons resolution *before the tax became law*; in 1961 the Treasury acquired power to vary almost any existing customs or excise duty by 10 per cent. In the face of this even the legal control of Parliament is wearing thin: the conventional doctrines of the British Constitution must be thought out anew. A government which can obtain

C   19

funds so easily is obviously in a different position from one which cannot.

The weakening control of Parliament over the government was strikingly confirmed in August 1966 when the government announced the appointment of a Parliamentary Commissioner (Ombudsman) not only before the bill creating that office had been passed but before it had even been discussed.

3

INSTITUTIONS

In the analysis of State institutions at least nine functions may be discerned. These are interdependent in various ways and the separation between them differs in character and distance from State to State. The distinction between them is to some extent artificial – the creation of the mind – and in the following pages they are not mentioned in an order of importance.

A. *Customs and habits.* Firstly, there must be established customs, habits of thought and behaviour. These tend to be embodied in a customary law handed down from the past, and they enshrine the way in which innovations are regarded. The special institution associated with this complex of ideas is the law court; the legal expression of the ideas themselves is called Common Law in England and Civil Law in Scotland, and they fill in the gaps where no written rules happen to exist; they are, so to speak, in reserve. The ideas are passive in the sense that law courts do not lead but act only when a dispute is brought before them, and in the sense also that disputes are only decided by reference to them if no higher law exists. On the other hand they are immensely important because they depend on permanent principles applicable (sometimes oddly) in all situations, whereas other laws tend to deal with special cases only.

B. *Machinery for change.* Secondly, there must be machinery for altering the rules when required. People's needs and behaviour are constantly changing and the rate of change seems to be increasing. There must be a means, short of violence,

21

whereby laws can be altered, services and institutes abolished, created or modified and money obtained by lawful means for the financing of public projects. The characteristic machine for doing all this by agreement is the legislature or Parliament by whose decrees all the citizens have (within reasonable limits) bound themselves to abide. As we have seen, the kingdom contains five of these: the Parliament at Westminster and the sub-legislatures in Ulster and the three islands. Theoretically – that is, in law – the Westminster Parliament can do anything: it can abolish the sub-legislatures or convert every church into a beer house. In reality there are important practical limits upon its theoretical powers: these limits are imposed primarily by time factors, and by the patience and the resources of the people. The powers of the sub-legislatures are limited by the supremacy of the Westminster Parliament and also by custom and specific rules, but their practical limitations do not differ in kind from those of their superior.

c. *Government*. To make changes by a smooth, lawful and coherent process there must be someone with the function of taking the initiative; there must, that is to say, be a channel by which proposals can be effectively made to the legislature. It is desirable that these should not contradict each other but should have some mutual relationship, and so there must be a body whose business it is to form a policy for the nation. A policy is an intention to achieve certain chosen ends, and with them in mind the policy maker will himself make proposals and will, in addition, judge of the consistency with them of proposals made by anyone else. The institution concerned with this function is usually called the Government. In London its head is called the Prime Minister; there are a number of other ministers and their subordinates (totalling about one hundred and ten) and of these the most influential meet as an organized committee called the Cabinet to discuss and decide the policy.

d. *Elections*. Now it is obvious that if the policy maker, that

22

is the government, wishes to achieve its purposes it must persuade Parliament to make the changes needed, and that therefore a working harmony of opinion must be achieved between Government and Parliament. In practice this means that a preponderance (in power) of those who sit in Parliament must agree with the Ministers. The fourth element, therefore, in the system is the method by which this harmony is achieved. In the United Kingdom this is done by holding periodical elections whose purpose is to appoint some 630 representatives of the nation to sit in the House of Commons. The contenders for these 630 seats are organized into political parties who profess differing but supposedly coherent opinions on national policy, and it is generally the leaders of the party which secures the most seats in the House of Commons who form the government. The members of this government are nearly all members of one or other House of Parliament.

E. *Liberty*. Very closely connected with the fourth or electoral element is a fifth which is 'liberty'. The electors cannot choose sensibly – or at all – if they and candidates cannot express opinions freely and if they cannot vote as they please. Freedom from molestation, from censorship and from abuse of power is essential to the working of the Constitution, but mere statements of this principle are not enough. There must be practical means of enforcing these freedoms and of repelling and punishing infringements. This is done primarily through the law courts and through the watchfulness of members of Parliament and the Press.

F. *Instruments*. Sixthly, if policies have been proposed and changes agreed, there must be a central organization for converting the decisions of Parliament into reality; for instance, if it has been decided that there shall be a national health service there must be someone to decide the distribution of the hospitals and place the building contracts. This is done mostly by the specialized government departments which are called

23

ministries; these are staffed by permanent and variously paid officials, but the head of each is a political minister who is a member of the policy-making government. Thus policy making and policy enforcement are in almost the same hands and tend to be confused. There is no necessary reason for this, but the practical reasons are strong: the formation of policy requires information which it will be the departments' business to obtain. Most of the same information will again be needed when the policy, having been agreed in whole or part, is to be carried out; but sometimes, nevertheless, a special type of body which is not a government department will be created to carry out a policy. Amongst such bodies are the boards of nationalized industries.

G. *Administration.* Seventhly, there must be ways of carrying out at the local level the policies which have been decided and planned at the capital. As a matter of fact these differ as between the divisions of the kingdom and also they involve the use of a great variety of officials, bodies, corporations and institutions endowed with functions based upon no logical pattern save perhaps a preference for specialization. In this realm of local administration it is a mistake to simplify what is in fact a complicated situation, but the institutions of local administration can be broadly classified into regional bodies, local branches of central ministries, local elected councils such as city corporations exercising a selection of powers conferred by law, other local bodies such as Water Resources Boards administering particular services and the local offshoots of nationalized industries.

H. *Taxation and Recruitment.* In any organized community there must be an effective method of withdrawing from private hands enough resources for the common use to enable the policies to be carried out. This entails two equally important operations: on the one hand there must be a way of collecting taxes which really will procure the money needed and on the

24

other there must be means to recruit the public servants necessary to do the work. Taxation is more often remembered than recruitment, but both are vital and complementary to each other. In wartime this becomes more obvious than in peace and recruitment is then secured by compulsion not merely for the forces, but for all activities necessary to the war effort.

I. *The Sovereign.* Lastly there must be an independent symbol which will engage the affection or loyalty of all or nearly all the people, even those who object to the policy of the government of the moment. The reason for this is that if loyalty is directed exclusively to a party and its policy, any party government will encounter violent and sometimes armed opposition from those not in power, and this might disrupt the business of the nation and eventually lead to the final disaster of civil war. Britain has been lucky in that it has experienced no civil war for three centuries, but European countries have suffered such murderous and destructive upheavals at frequent intervals in the present century. In this country the symbol of the nation's unity is the Sovereign: other countries have other symbols, most of which seem to be psychologically weaker.

The foregoing description has listed nine of the main characteristics of government as if they were separate and functionally unrelated conceptions, but it would be an error to suppose that they were as widely separated as any analysis tends to suggest. Thus the Sovereign in fact takes part in the formulation of policy as well as functioning as a living symbol. The courts administer new law – the product of change – as well as old custom. Policy is conditioned by availability of trained manpower or by the inability or refusal of taxpayers to pay up; and custom is the foundation of liberty. Every part of the Constitution reacts in some way upon every other.

25

4

INFLUENCES

A constitution consists of a series of groups of people. These conduct public business in accordance with rules only some of which are rules of law, and each member of one of the governing groups has associates and contacts which react far out into society. Constitutions do not exist in the air: unless there are people to work them they do not exist at all; their most important element is human and a description of the law, the rules and the governing bodies alone would resemble an account of an iceberg which failed to mention water.

A. *People.* Modern government involves a huge number of daily detailed operations, and governments directly employ in various capacities both high and low a very large number of people. These include whole office blocks full of typists, accounts clerks, messengers, doorkeepers and chauffeurs. A serious shortage of these people may hold up the execution of important decisions: the delays, for instance, in the presentation of the first plan to reorganize Wales was caused in part by printing difficulties. Individually these people may not be specially important: but in the mass they are essential and, because of their numbers, very expensive.

B. *Civil Servants.* At a higher level there is a solid layer of civil servants of various grades. These are comparatively well and sometimes very well paid; in the upper levels they are carefully recruited, well educated and trained and clever and well-informed. They are becoming increasingly powerful because they have more information than anyone else and it is to them that ministers must come for advice and facts. Their power rests mainly (but not wholly) on their ability to 'make a case' and their constant presence in all government deliberations. The Minister may be the head of the ministry, but when he returns from a debate in Parliament he has to face the personality of his chief civil servant who knows more than he does, and who is permanent while he is not.

c. *Politicians*. Next in order there is a shifting group of politicians. This includes all the members of the House of Commons, the more active peers, a number of paid and unpaid party officials, and some people who for various reasons are temporarily out of Parliament. In many cases the wives must be included in this group. Politicians derive their influence from their connection with the public – all 56 million members of it – and with public opinion. Amongst themselves their influence depends upon a surprising variety of factors: one may be remarkable for his brains or wit; another because he happens to be a television personality; a third because a successful career in trade unionism has given him the backing of a powerful organization. There are members of the House of Commons who seldom say a word and others to whom no one listens; and there are influential political figures who exercise their magic almost wholly in private.

d. *Parties*. The connecting link between the politician and public opinion is the political party, that is, the organized body of people who hold the same opinions as he does and who find the money, the arguments and the active workers to persuade the electors to vote for him. Just as a civil service has its typists, so a political party has its low-level workers, but the difference is that the latter are unpaid. The success of a given political idea depends mostly on the numbers who are willing to work for it voluntarily; if all these volunteers turn against a politician his chances of remaining in office become slim. If

27

the politician's power resides in his ability to say what people want, the influence of the party is based on the toleration of the party worker.

E. *Mass media.* The existence of parties is made possible by the circulation of political ideas; the media of mass communication, the newspapers, radio, television, cinemas, theatres and the advertising industry are essential components of the system. Those who direct (but not necessarily those who own) these great institutions must be counted amongst the most powerful of the policy makers and at one period enormous power was wielded single-handed by *The Times*. Nowadays their influence is seldom exerted directly or in ways or on issues which one might expect. The fact that most of the Press was conservative did not prevent the landslide Labour victory after the Second World War. For every person who is convinced by a direct statement there is another who reacts against it: the public influence of the Press is more strongly felt in the atmosphere which it creates than in the pronouncements it makes. Perhaps the most important contribution to politics made by the mass media recently is the magnification of the personalities of the party leaders. The names and faces of these three men are far better known than those of their colleagues or indeed than the principles for which their parties respectively claim to stand.

A lesser, but important contribution is the currency which the mass media give through correspondence columns, interviews and so forth to opinions held by private persons. This has to some extent compensated for the disappearance of the independent Member of Parliament.

F. *Business.* Since everyone has to eat, organizations concerned with business or employment are closely involved with politics where they have affiliations with political parties as well as exerting a certain independent leverage; the effective power in the growing industrial combines is in the possession

28

of the managers not the shareholders, and as one might expect the weapon of the business community is its knowledge of and capacity for management and its ability to manipulate capital. The complementary power of labour is its capacity through trades unions to bring business to a halt by means of strikes.

The effectiveness of strikes depends on the ability of the strikers to sustain themselves and their families. In a period of very full employment they may get other jobs; if less lucky they may have to depend upon the union's funds, until they in turn run out. The striker's position has been accidentally strengthened by P.A.Y.E. for as his unemployment lengthens his tax liability declines until he is entitled to the return of tax overpaid.

Speaking very roughly the employers are associated with the Conservative, and the trade unions with the Labour parties, while the Liberals by attempting to represent consumers appeal to both rich and poor in their capacity as buyers of goods and services. It would, however, be an over-simplification to accept this as a complete picture: businessmen are found at all levels of the Labour Party; the Tories could never reach power without the support of many trade unionist voters, and the Co-operative movement, which is in one sense a consumers' organization, is closely linked with the Labour Party.

G. *Organizations.* There are, seventhly, a very large number of organizations concerned with specialized interests. Individually these exert influence only in connection with their own specialization which may be a major or a minor matter, but as governments commonly consult such bodies when their field is likely to be invaded by policy, it follows that they exert (separately or in alliance) a strong influence if only through the power of delay. Moreover, such groups have spokesmen in Parliament in the form of individual members whom they have persuaded to take part in their work and to protect their interests. These organizations are extremely varied; they range from professional bodies such as the Bar Council and the

Institute of Chartered Accountants to federations of allotment holders and amateur anglers, and include associations of local authorities, headmasters, and churches of all faiths. Their influence is in its nature (though not in its power) somewhere between that of a civil service and that of the politicians, for within their specialization they, like the civil service, have unrivalled knowledge, but like the politicians they represent a body of public opinion. It is inconceivable, for instance, that in a public issue which turned on a technical question of medicine any government would wholly ignore the unanimous opinion of the heads of the great medical colleges.

The techniques of pressure exerted by employers and labour organizations and by the specialist bodies vary a good deal according to circumstances and taste. Mostly quiet methods (such as the confidential talk and the private or official letter) are preferred, but as the stakes increase the 'noise level' will rise. Delegations, protest meetings, petitions, and letter-writing campaigns may be launched, and at moments of great crisis there may be processions. The correct measure of pressure to use is a matter of very nice judgement, for constant or unreasonable overplaying destroys public or official sympathy, while underplaying may not be audible in the general hubbub.

H. *Universities.* A different type of influence is exercised by the universities. These great and growing corporations of learned men train many people who become constitutionally influential later on, and in this sense their power is felt at long range. Independently of this educational function, however, they engage in research, the amassing of information for its own sake and the formation of theories arising from their discoveries. In the social, political and economic spheres with which government is concerned, this mental activity is growing and the members of institutions such as All Souls and Nuffield Colleges at Oxford, and the London School of Economics are well known in political quarters. In one sense this class of opinion is irresponsible – that is to say that academic solutions of public problems are propounded by people who will not themselves necessarily have to carry them out. As a result they do not usually win quick acceptance but are injected into the bloodstream of the body politic where they may circulate covertly for years before creating a visible reaction. Nevertheless their direct influence has increased and continues to do so.

I. *Individuals*. Lastly there are the influential individuals. These and the sectors where their power is felt vary greatly from time to time. It is unwise to ignore their existence yet difficult to be sure who they are or why they carry the weight they do. It was largely through Duff Cooper's personal efforts as ambassador in Paris that the import duty on French wine was reduced: this happened because his personal influence was greater than that of his office. Florence Nightingale revolutionized the hospitals and nursing services through her personal example in the Crimean War. The Earl of Shaftesbury produced a complete change in the national outlook on the care of children and if no one now remembers William Willett, the originator of Summer Time, it will be long before the names of Wolfenden and of Beeching are forgotten.

5

THE 5000

From the influences at work in the management of the nation it is possible – roughly – to infer the number and type of people who actually have a part in it. The number is quite small: five thousand at the outside. They are, obviously, not of equal permanent importance nor is their relative power constant. Some, such as ministers, make the decisions; some, such as civil servants, have direct access to the decision-makers, and some influence the way the rest behave and think. The importance of an individual is determined partly by office or position but quite as much by character, health, background or the relevance of a particular situation or expertise to a major issue of the period. Much also depends upon width of acquaintanceship and ability to convince, on manners and manner as well as logic and knowledge. Parnell was ruined by a divorce case; as a scientist professor Lindemann greatly influenced the direction of the Second World War; the plays of George Bernard Shaw eroded the political confidence of the Edwardians; and George V established the principle that the Premier should be in the Commons by preferring Baldwin to Curzon.

Membership is necessarily mobile; people will be drawn in or driven out by a variety of circumstances not invariably political; it follows that 'The 5000' is a name or symbolic figure (like 'hundredweight') and that there is, besides, an indeterminate number who were once in and may return or who will probably be drawn in and know it. There is also an important distinction between a member's qualifications and the actual leverage which he exercises. A few reach eminence only as delegates or mouthpieces for the interests or constituences which they represent, and are heard for no other reason. Most affect the potential influence of their own 'interests' by the way they act, and usually bend the policies of their masters by the manner in which they report back to them. A negotiator's private estimate of the possibilities is a powerful influence over the decisions of his principals. Most of The 5000 are, so to speak, set apart: they owe a loyalty to the attitude or interest which they represent but the need to fit it into a larger picture creates another loyalty to something more important as well. Burke's doctrine that a Member of Parliament owes a duty to the nation transcending his duty to his constituents applies similarly, but not always in the same fashion, to everyone in public life except perhaps the Sovereign. It is the essence of a politics of compromise that every politician must serve at least two masters.

A necessary feature of The 5000, following from its collective characteristics, is that it is not an 'establishment'. Quite the reverse. It is fluid rather than static, and far from being monolithic its members are often in acute (and in the past, mortal) conflict not only on policies but on the very composition of The 5000 itself and on the way in which its members go about their business and settle their differences. This is the machine of public affairs; the power is generated by the heat within. The 5000, their interrelationships and the rules and practices governing them and their conflicts are the constitution.

The following, then, is one attempt to estimate the present composition of The 5000, this is to say the numbers of individuals. The reader may reach a different conclusion. The figures, of course, give no clue to the relative importance of the various classes or persons included.

1. Crown and Court.   10
2. M.P.s and Active Peers. This group includes the
   ministers.   900
3. Those high public officials upon whom ministers lean
   directly for information and advice together with a
   number of senior officials who are habitually called

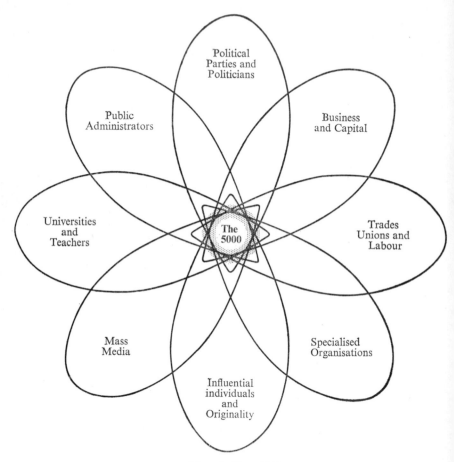

Fig. 3. THE 5000

The 'petals' represent masses of people, but they overlap in the same way as most people have more than one interest. As you get nearer the centre the number gets fewer and fewer and the overlapping increasingly elaborate until the centre is reached. Some eccentrics however overshoot the centre through overemphasis or fanaticism.

34

in. This group includes parliamentary clerks, civil servants paid £5,000 a year and about half those paid slightly less, and the members and principal servants of the boards of nationalized industries. 500

4. Religious leaders, i.e. the bishops of the Anglican and Roman Churches and the leading personalities in other denominations in the United Kingdom. 100
5. Armed Services and Police. 30
6. Local Government. This group includes a number of influential leaders of the Local Authority Associations. 50
7. Lawyers. (Members of the Law Commission, well-known judges and magistrates, chairmen of the Bar Council, Law Society and Magistrates Association.) 50
8. Academics and Research Bodies. This group includes well-known professors in the fields of economics, sociology, and administration; fellows of colleges related to these subjects, and interested foundations. 150
9. Educational. This group includes influential experts, some heads of schools, H.M.I.s, professors in University Departments of Education. 50
10. Professional Organizations and Clubs (e.g. the Institute of Chartered Accountants; some major Livery Companies; the British Medical Association). 100
11. Television and Broadcasting. 30
12. London (National) Press. 30
13. Other Press. 30
14. Advertising. 20
15. Theatre and Cinema. 25
16. Individual Publicists (Authors, Playwrights, Journalists and Broadcasters). 200
17. National Voluntary Organizations (e.g. the Womens' Institutes, Civic Trust, National Council of Social Service). 50
18. Employers, Industrialists and Shipowners. 300
19. Trades Unions. 100
20. Banks, and Insurance. 50
21. Friendly and Building Societies. 50
22. Agriculture. 25
23. Charitable Bodies and Foundations (e.g. City Parochial, Carnegie, Nuffield, Gulbenkian, Dartington). 50

24. Miscellaneous individuals.   50
25. Political party officials (central offices).   25
26. Constituency party officials and agents (i.e. the leading local personality in the party holding a constituency, plus opposite numbers in marginal areas).   800
27. Foreigners. This group includes ambassadors, e.g. of U.S.A., U.S.S.R., France, West Germany; representatives of international organizations and certain foreign banks; directors of foreign oil companies, and so forth.   100

	3,875
Less 10 per cent for overlapping	385
	3,490
28. Add wives or husbands	1,240
	± 4,730

Wives or husbands are included because they affect public life in two particular ways. Some directly influence events by their own talents and public actions. Others produce a strong effect upon their partners. It is necessarily hard to estimate their numbers but observation seems to show that in religious and political activities the proportion is high; in administration and business negligible and in the rest moderate.

6

CUSTOM AND COMMON LAW

The earliest purpose and primary object of government is to keep order, because little constructive or profitable activity is possible if private energies have to be largely diverted to self-defence. Crime on a big scale, habitual disorder and civil war are only different degrees of a social malady which impoverishes the citizens and sometimes leads to mass starvation.

The experience of this led early societies to develop a commonly held opinion about the proper way to live. This opinion would differ from one place or tribe to another and it was seldom (if ever) exactly defined, but practical needs soon brought two institutions into existence. The first was some method of putting an end to violence when it had already broken out; the second a way of preventing it from breaking out at all. The first led to the 'police idea'; the second to a publicly recognized means of settling disputes. The first is the foundation of the criminal law; the other the origin of the civil law. Both require someone who can say what the law is.

The nature of law has been disputed for centuries, but one thing seems clear. The first efforts to establish order were efforts to make the violent or rebellious live in accordance with locally accepted opinion of what was right and proper. A man either lived as his neighbours lived or (in the empty state of the early world) went away and lived somewhere else or got into serious trouble. Early history shows many cases of exile.

Very soon it was found that there might be a dispute on whether a given act was right and proper. The ancients did not think in terms of *making* laws, partly one suspects, because they could not write. Their concern was to discover a rule which was believed to exist already; right and proper conduct was the result of wisdom and knowledge. A dispute was submitted to a wise man of standing who settled the case in accordance with his knowledge and any deductions which he could make from it. As it was not thought fair to decide two similar disputes differently a habit of applying the same rulings to similar cases grew up. Slowly over the centuries a body of decisions came to be recognized as laws; thus custom announced through the mouths of judges became a recognizable collection of rules known in England as the Common Law.

Custom is not, however, confined to the formal domain of law. It will be found in many branches of ordinary life and government. It is normal for civil servants to look up the precedents before reaching a decision, and the Speaker of the House of Commons habitually does so. This national habit is a formidable obstacle both to arbitrary government and to enterprise.

Now private violence was not regarded as wrong so much as publicly inconvenient. If a judge refused to settle a case the aggrieved man might still take his rights by force: in other words the inconvenience would result – and this inconvenience might also be an injustice if a powerful man made a false claim against a weak one. The judge, therefore, had, in the public interest, to be ready to settle any dispute about anything, and as his decisions had to be mutually consistent, the Common Law had to develop principles which could always be applied. This is its situation today: it is in theory a body of principles based on the settlement of actual cases and applicable (in the absence of any other rule) to every dispute brought before a judge.

Originally the Common Law dealt with primitive situations, but as history moved on it became more sophisticated. As might be expected in a method which was developed through experience some of its principles were more durable than others. For instance, justice requires that both sides in a dispute shall have an equal opportunity to state their case because otherwise the judge will not have before him all the material necessary for his decision; such a principle is always true and is sometimes called the 'Rule of Natural Justice'. On the other hand a rule that the Lords of certain lands must in time of war provide an armed horseman to serve in the army has little relevance in the atomic era. As it happens English (but not Scots) law regards legal rules as permanent unless altered by lawful process. Judges know the law but do not make it. In the absence of any way of altering things the Lords of the Manors would still be providing lancers now.

Changing circumstances thus bring into the open a need to make, that is to say to change law. Such new laws are embodied in Acts of Parliament or statutes which are in writing. The most important, though not the most noticed feature of a written law is that it deals with a subject which is limited by its own purpose and words. Wherever some matter is untouched by a statute it will be governed by the Common Law which remains permanently in reserve.

Somewhere between the Common Law and the Statutes which change the law there will be found an important body of mostly old Acts which purport to declare the Common Law in statute form. These Acts are important historically because they mark the transition from law-speaking to law-making and, as it happens, one of them is Magna Carta which is important on its own account. It is instructive that it was thought necessary to reaffirm or re-enact this fundamental document over thirty times in the course of the Middle Ages. It took a long time to establish the idea of made law.

Despite inroads, the Common Law is still very important in the field of government. The existence of the Crown, the form of Parliament and the laws, customs and usages of the constitution are founded upon it; its rules govern the interpretation of statutes and set out many of the limitations on the powers of authority. Perhaps the most important single rule of all, the so called 'Rule of Law', is a doctrine of the Common Law. Stated simply this requires that no one can be molested or disturbed in his person or property except by authority of

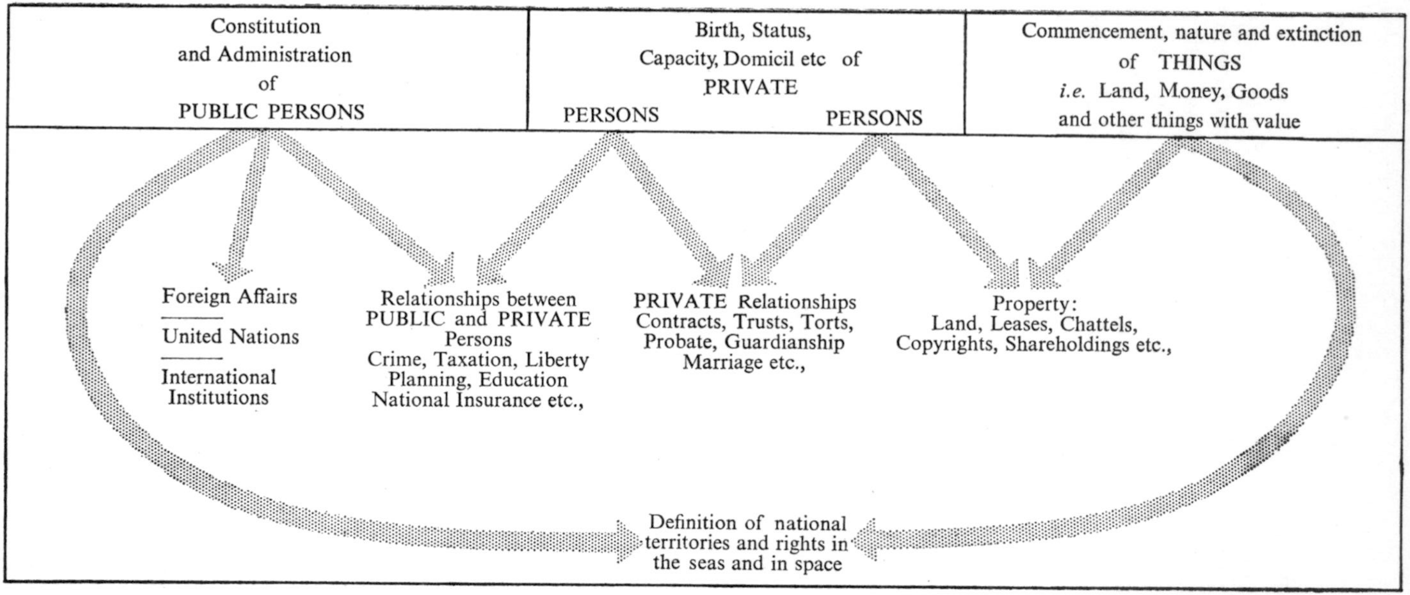

Fig. 4. SCHEME OF LEGAL IDEAS

Constitution and Administration of PUBLIC PERSONS	Birth, Status, Capacity, Domicil etc of PRIVATE PERSONS	Commencement, nature and extinction of THINGS *i.e.* Land, Money, Goods and other things with value

PERSONS

Foreign Affairs
United Nations
International Institutions

Relationships between PUBLIC and PRIVATE Persons
Crime, Taxation, Liberty Planning, Education National Insurance etc.,

PRIVATE Relationships
Contracts, Trusts, Torts, Probate, Guardianship Marriage etc.,

Property:
Land, Leases, Chattels, Copyrights, Shareholdings etc.,

Definition of national territories and rights in the seas and in space the law itself. This is very far-reaching in all private and public affairs. In private matters, for instance, it is the principle behind the law of landed property and the right of people of full age to manage their own affairs. In public law it protects personal liberty through the celebrated writ of Habeas Corpus by requiring anyone who restricts another's liberty to produce a lawful authority for so doing; it prevents the levy of any tax not authorized or defined by Parliament and by a logical extension it requires compensation to be paid for any property which is taken compulsorily for public use.

It is sometimes said that this paramount principle of the Rule of Law has been extensively eroded in the past century by the passage of successive statutes conferring wide discretions on various public authorities, and in this there is undoubtedly some truth; for instance the law of planning prevents a landowner from doing what he will with his land, and the Treasury can within certain limits vary customs duties. Nevertheless it is still true that English government cannot be understood without constant reference to the Rule. Such freedom of choice and action as exists can only be restricted by the enactment of new statutes, and references, mostly implied rather than explicit, to this state of affairs will be found scattered throughout the rest of this book.

Part Two

THE MACHINE OF SOVEREIGNTY

7

THE CROWN AND GOVERNMENT

Sovereignty is sometimes used as a technical term expressing the unlimited legal power to do anything. Some States (for instance the United States of America) have written constitutions which limit the powers of government and legislature. In such a case it is doubtful where sovereignty resides or even whether there is a 'sovereign' at all. In the United Kingdom there is no such constitutional document and sovereignty is vested without doubt in a composite institution, namely, the Crown (whose wearer is also sometimes called the sovereign), the House of Lords and the House of Commons in Parliament assembled. Each of these components has certain limited powers of its own, but none by itself can exercise the functions of a sovereign. Moreover, these functions can be exercised only in accordance with parliamentary law. The Crown, for instance, has the exclusive right to call a parliament into existence: if the two Houses assembled without a summons from the Crown and passed bills in apparently proper form to which the Crown gave its assent, the proceedings would be a nullity because the assembly would not be Parliament.

A draft law when laid before Parliament is called a bill. Bills to which the Crown and Parliament have agreed are called Acts of Parliament or sometimes Statutes. These can theoretically effect anything however important or trivial, wise or unwise, just or unjust, reasonable or unreasonable. The Statute of Westminster 1931 made Canada, Australia, New Zealand and South Africa into independent States; by the Round Oak Steel Works (Level Crossings) Act, 1959, the company of that name is entitled to divert a crossing over Level Street, Brierley Hill; the

45

Earl of Strafford was put to death without trial in 1641 under an Act of Attainder which applied only to him; the Corn Laws, until their repeal in 1846, prevented the import of corn until prices reached almost famine level; the National Health Service Acts make medical care available to all.

Though the three parts have different rights and functions their essential unity as a single machine is secured by a number of interlocking devices. Except in special cases (to be mentioned later) an Act requires the consent of all three and a bill involving taxation or expenditure must be originated by the Crown and introduced in the House of Commons. These two rules are reinforced by a further one that every bill must pass all its stages in the course of a single session – that is to say within usually about a year. The combined effect is that (with one notable exception) bills must be very thoroughly discussed and that there is time for only a limited number of them. This restraint was partly evaded in 1966–7 by having no autumn prorogation.

The Crown and its Advisers

The Crown is a common law office but is vested by Acts of Parliament in the descendants of the Electress Sophia of Hanover (who died in 1714 and was a granddaughter of King James I) other than the Duke of Windsor and his descendants if any. It passes from a reigning monarch to his or her children, princes being preferred to princesses and the elder to the younger. If the monarch is childless it goes to the descendants (in the same order) of the previous monarch nearest in time who had children.

The reigning Sovereign is paid no salary and pays no taxes. The immense Crown Estates produce an income so huge that they far exceed any possible needs of the Crown, and since the latter part of the 18th Century an agreement has been made at the beginning of each reign whereby the Crown Estates are managed by commissioners; these pay the income into the Treasury which in return pays a fixed annual sum called the

Civil List for the support of the Monarch. The resulting profit to the taxpayers is very large.

The Monarch's legal powers are derived from two sources: 'prerogative', which is the royal part of the Common Law, and 'statute'. They are very extensive indeed; they include, as already mentioned, the power to summon and dismiss Parliament, to appoint and dismiss ministers and other public servants, to manage foreign policy, conclude treaties and wage wars, to appoint members of the House of Lords, and judges and to create corporations and universities. No money can be paid out of the Treasury and no bishop of the Established Church can be elected without royal authority. The Monarch is the chief person in the land, the undoubted head of the State and the fountain of all honours and precedence. The Sovereign cannot be personally impleaded in any court and it is treason to attempt to overthrow the Crown or to kill its holder.

The enormous legal powers of the Crown are (with two important but rare exceptions) no longer exercised by the Sovereign on his or her own responsibility. All government requires money and the ability to wield force, but the legal power over taxation and the army is in the hands of Parliament; the Monarch's powers are effectually controlled through the parliamentary machine because it could refuse to pay for a policy which it disliked. This is the lynch pin of parliamentary control of the Monarch.

In fact the powers of government are exercised upon the formal advice of the Prime Minister who must be in a position to assure the Monarch that the course of action advised is one which Parliament will support. The Prime Minister therefore always has at his command the most votes in the House of Commons and all normal acts of government are done by the Monarch in pursuance of his advice. The Prime Minister therefore actually exercises the powers of the Crown so long as but no longer than he retains the support of Parliament. The result is an inversion of the theory: Prime Ministers come and go but the Crown never dies: a Monarch is the Prime Minister's best informed, and after a few years on the throne his most experienced adviser.

Apart from the conferment of certain very high honours there are two great powers in the exercise of which the crown is not fettered by advice. Firstly a monarch is not bound to accept advice to dissolve a parliament and hold new elections simply because a Prime Minister cannot command parliamentary support: instead someone else can be invited to take office and form a government. The second case is that the Crown is not bound to accept advice on the identity of the next Prime Minister; ordinarily it will be obvious who he should be, but special cases do arise where the prerogative must be personally exercised as, for instance, where a Prime Minister dies in office, or where there is a balance of political parties or where at a crucial juncture no obvious leader was available in the ranks of the parliamentary majority. The appointment of Asquith on the death of Campbell-Bannerman in 1908 is an example of the first kind; the choice of Baldwin in 1923 in preference to the Marquess Curzon of the last. The appearance in politics of the television-made party leader may perhaps have rendered the latter use of the power obsolete.

The Privy Council

Nowadays the ancient Privy Council exists mainly for formal reasons but it still has important characteristics. Membership is conferred upon ministers and as a high honour upon persons not involved in British politics, and it is the Privy Councillor's oath which binds Cabinet ministers to keep policy matters secret. Membership confers prestige, and its Lord President is always a very senior member of the government and sometimes deputy Prime Minister. In the House of Commons membership confers a customary right to speak in priority to others; in view of the size of the membership and the shortage of debating time this is not a negligible privilege; in important debates it is difficult for a back-bencher to secure a hearing.

In addition to this it has two valuable functional purposes. As a disengaged body it is the cradle of ministerial experiments. The oldest of these is the Judicial Committee which has sat since Tudor times as the final court of appeal from overseas territories; the Board of Trade is a committee of the Privy Council instituted in the 17th Century (it never meets); the department of education began similarly in the 19th and coalesced with a department of science which grew out of it in the 20th.

The other function is that it acts as a secondary formal channel of advice to the Sovereign who wields a large number of powers through the use of Orders in Council. These vary in importance from the proclamation of a blockade in wartime to the closure of a churchyard. In practice each is made on the representation of a specialist minister; in a major matter he will have secured the support of the Cabinet: in a minor one he will make the proposal on his own. The procedure by way of the Privy Council is a convenient means of taking work off the shoulders of the Prime Minister.

The membership of the Privy Council is very large (316 in 1966) but it never meets as a whole. Its individual members are summoned as required for consideration of the particular matters in hand.

The Cabinet

The Cabinet began in the early 1700s as an informal gathering of influential Privy Councillors meeting without the King, who spoke no English and was often away in Hanover. It has become the most powerful element in the whole constitution, but is in its turn dominated by the Prime Minister who, by way of advice to the Sovereign, appoints and dismisses all its members. The number of these varies in peace-time from eighteen to twenty-five, but in the two world wars the numbers were much smaller. All the members are senior ministers (though not necessarily ministers with departmental responsibilities) but there are also ministers who are not members. The

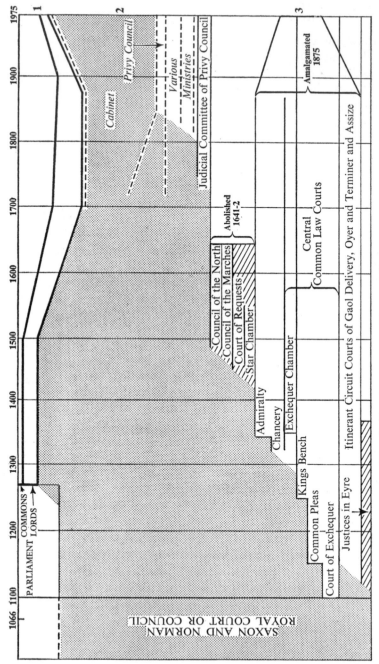

Fig. 5. Development of English Institutions

This illustrates the way most English institutions (other than Parliament) have grown out of the government. The tendency of the components to develop at each other's expense is indicated by variations in the width of the sections. Only the major institutions are included.

Cabinet's deliberations are secret and its decisions are reached by consensus or agreement: it is said never to vote. The Prime Minister presides and decides what shall be discussed. In general it meets once a week, and it has committees for special purposes, such as a legislative committee to decide what bills should be introduced or supported in Parliament and in what order of priority; and it has at its disposal a small body of the very scarce legal parliamentary draftsmen.

The Cabinet (and all other ministers) automatically go out of office when the Prime Minister resigns, but despite his dominance the Cabinet is collectively responsible for the government's policy; a Cabinet minister who disagrees with his colleagues must either defer to them, or persuade them or resign.

The great power of the Cabinet comes from a variety of interdependent sources. Its members are well known and often famous; most of them will carry great weight within their party; they are well informed through the ministries and the Cabinet Secretariat; but the primary source of their power is their ability to command (in the most literal manner) the actions of their supporters in the House of Commons. This is done through the Government Whips.

Non-Cabinet and Junior Ministers and Departmental Preoccupation

Apart from Cabinet ministers there are ministers who are the political heads of departments but who are not in the Cabinet, and in addition every head of a department whether in the Cabinet or not has one or more paid junior ministers. The junior to a Secretary of State is called the Parliamentary Under-Secretary of State; that of a minister is called the Parliamentary Secretary. Sometimes also there are Ministers of State who are usually grander (and better paid) than other junior ministers. Most ministers (whether departmental heads or juniors) have a member of their own House attached to them, who is called the minister's Parliamentary Private Secretary, and who is unpaid.

E   51

In all, these amount to a considerable percentage of the majority party; in the Commons, of 320 Labour Members in the Parliament elected in 1964, seventy-two held paid offices and a further twenty-eight acted as parliamentary private secretaries. A mere handful of these were in the Lords. Thus about 30 per cent of the majority party or 15 per cent of the Members of the Commons were wholly or mainly engaged in specialist work, and had a foot on a rung of the ladder of ambition. Every increase in the number of such rungs adds to the power of the Prime Minister over his party.

The Whips and Public Opinion

Every parliamentary party needs someone to ensure that its members act consistently with the party policy. That someone is the 'whip', who in the first place exercises his peculiar function by translating the policy into a series of directions to members on how they shall vote or not vote. Ordinarily these directions (which are also confusingly called 'whips') will be obeyed because the members will be in general agreement with their party leaders, but, as usual, the situation is more complicated than this. The party leaders, especially those on the government side who as a Cabinet deliberate in secret, need to know the limits of the policies which their party is prepared to support and must ensure that their supporters properly understand them. Hence within parliamentary parties there are specialist committees to focus back-benchers' opinions and to convey them to ministers, and conversely when an issue of importance or difficulty has to be decided a minister will explain the policy to such a committee meeting in private.

The effect of the party committee system is to reduce the occasions when back-benchers have to obey written whips which they dislike, and helps to ensure that unpopular policies are understood and supported. Nevertheless cases do occur where members have doubts about the wisdom of the government to which they have been pledged and it is in this that the special skill of the whip shows itself. Some have to be won by diplomacy or appeals to loyalty or ambition; others may have to be bullied into toeing the line by direct or inferential reference to the ultimate threat of 'withdrawal of the whip' – a polite term for expulsion.

The effect of this withdrawal is that the member is no longer entitled to attend any of the party meetings; he receives nothing through the party research organization; he will not be recommended for honours; his supporters and voluntary workers in his constituency will be encouraged to desert him, and probably his party will sponsor a rival candidate at the next election. Obviously from a member's point of view a course of action leading to withdrawal of the whip is a serious matter, but from the party's point of view the act of withdrawal is serious too: it may be possible to expel a single individual but wholesale expulsions will merely create a new and independent party out of the expelled. A concerted threat by a substantial group of members to vote against their own party can have far-reaching results especially (but not exclusively) if the majority in the Commons is a small one. In 1940 such a threat was carried out and led to the replacement of Chamberlain by Churchill, even though Chamberlain in fact secured a vote of support in the House.

Thus the ascendancy of the Cabinet inside the majority party is not absolute, but depends in the last analysis on its prestige: that is to say upon its believed ability to match up to the current situation. The creation and sustenance of such a prestige is the major preoccupation of the politicians.

In the modern era of mass organizations and mass media of communication, each respectively exerting pressures in various ways on each other and on the government of the moment, the management of public opinion is becoming an increasingly important feature of the technique of public affairs. The whips have their counterparts outside Westminster in the central offices of the great political parties. These maintain a network of contacts with organizations and newspapers favourable to their point of view; they seek to represent policy in a light which is agreeable to their purpose, or attempt to distract public attention from measures which are deemed necessary, but believed to be unpopular. It is perhaps (but not probably) a coincidence that the sensational findings of the Vassall inquiry into espionage were released to the Press at the moment when the unpopular Beeching proposals on the railways had just been published.

The Ministries

As physical civilization becomes more complex, more human activities seem to need government supervision; the means of doing this tend to be created when a need seems to have arisen and not in accordance with a plan, and it is greatly influenced by accidental factors. For instance, High Court judges are appointed by the Sovereign on the advice of the Lord Chancellor because they and he were crucially important in their respective spheres in the Middle Ages. Justices of the Peace, on the other hand, used to be* appointed through the Home Secretary because Tudor monarchs made them the instrument of local administration and the Secretary was the Minister responsible for supervising it at that time.

The ministries, then, show no specially coherent pattern and indeed one might discern in the sometimes illogical division of functions a desire to prevent too much power falling into the hands of any one of them. Nevertheless it is possible, for the sake of convenience, to attempt a rough classification.

For descriptive purposes this classification is based upon the ministries in London, but Northern Ireland, Man and the Channel Islands run their internal affairs with little interference, while Wales and Scotland each havé a Secretary of State with a department whose subdivisions correspond to and function locally in the same way as some of those London ministries concerned with internal matters.

* They are now appointed by the Lord Chancellor.

Firstly, there are the departments which deal with the internal management of the kingdom; these include the Home Office, the Ministry of Housing and Local Government, the Ministry of Land and Natural Resources, the Ministry of Transport and (in its anomalous fashion) the Post Office. Secondly, there are ministries dealing with the personal welfare of people: these include Social Security, Education and Science, and Health. Thirdly, there is a group concerned with external affairs: there are the Foreign and Commonwealth Offices, the Department of Technical Co-operation and the Ministry of Defence. Fourthly, there is a curious but important group of functionaries each of whom ostensibly exists for one purpose but in practice is used, as occasion arises, for another; these include the Lord President of the Council, the Lord Privy Seal, the Chancellor of the Duchy of Lancaster, the Minister without Portfolio, and the Paymaster-General. These appointments carry nominal or in the case of the Privy Seal no duties, and their holders are employed on such other high government business as happens to be important at the time. The Lord President was deputy Prime Minister in the Second World War; the Lord Privy Seal led the British side in the abortive Common Market negotiations in 1961–3; the Paymaster was the wartime chief scientific adviser to the government and the Minister without Portfolio was responsible for the Government's public relations in the Macmillan administration.

Lastly, there is the most influential group of all; the central ministries whose decisions affect all the others. These include the Lord Chancellor's small department, the Board of Trade, and the Department for Economic Affairs, but by far the most important of them is the Treasury. The nature of the Treasury points to its immense power: its civil servants are recruited from other ministries and never from outside. Its permanent civil service head is also the acknowledged Head of the Civil Service. Its political headship is vested in Lords Commissioners: of these the First Lord is the Prime Minister and the others are the government whips, while the Minister in charge of detailed Treasury business is the Chancellor of the Exchequer who is also responsible for laying the budget before the House of Commons.

Financial control of government affairs is mainly vested in the Treasury, though accounts and estimates are eventually scrutinized by committees of the House of Commons. As most other ministries depend on finance to carry out policies it follows that they cannot act save in consultation with Treasury officials at a lower level, and the Prime Minister and Chancellor of the Exchequer at the level of politics. On the other hand, the influence of the Treasury varies with the funds required from it; he who pays the piper usually but not always calls the tune. Administrative history has an important section which is concerned with the extent to which particular departments have – or have not – freed themselves from Treasury control. Some have self-balancing funds; others, especially the great spenders such as the Ministry of Defence, and the department of Education and Science, seem to be in a constant state of feud with the Treasury. The channel through which a ministry eventually brings pressure to bear is the Cabinet and the Prime Minister, but sometimes an appeal is made, outside the ambit of ordinary politics, directly to public opinion. Government departments are, after all, great corporations of people and, as anyone knows who steps inside one, they develop corporate personalities of their own and a dedication to their sense of purpose. They would be only human if sometimes they overstepped the limits of constitutional propriety in what to them is an important public interest. Thus some departmental committee reports read like manifestoes – which is what they are.

Civil Services

To obtain and interpret information, to match up the political intentions of the government party with the ascertained facts, to turn policies into public documents and to carry out the intentions of Parliament and Government, large staffs are required. Apart from the many run-of-the-mill office workers already mentioned, there is a need for people of the highest ability; the term 'civil servant' is often applied to these latter and embraces a number of distinct categories of officials – namely the Administrative Grade of the Civil Service, the Government Legal Service and various specialized groups of scientific workers. The total number of these very high grade public servants is small: in 1963 it was not much above 3,000. To this must be added the Foreign Service which, owing to its numerous outstations, is relatively much larger than the higher classes of the Civil Service.

All these high services are recruited through a fairly rigorous system of examination, inspection and selection. The abilities required are in short supply and the government must compete with other employers for the available talent. Consequently the services offer considerable security, and – at the top – salaries well above those of the ministers who are nominally in charge. Nowadays taxation is so high in the upper income brackets that a modest increase of spendable income can only be achieved by a very large increase of salary. To many, this does not warrant the extra exertions involved and other compensations for high office are very acceptable. Undoubtedly power for its own sake is an object of ambition; some of the work is highly satisfactory in its nature, and civil servants always receive a substantial share of each half-year's honours and decorations.

Commissions, Other Inquiries, and Studies

Sometimes a problem arises which requires government action, but is complex without being urgent. Preliminary detailed study in such cases is both desirable and possible, and it is a practice to institute working parties or committees of inquiry, or to set up a Royal Commission to inquire, report and make appropriate recommendations. Royal Commissions have power to compel witnesses and demand documents: the other bodies are less formal.

One seldom understood feature of Royal Commissions is that their members are mostly unpaid and so have to do their work on a part-time basis, while their staffs come from the civil service. Thus the speed and thoroughness of an investigation is controlled by the size of the funds and staff made available by the government.

Whatever their constitution the investigations of these bodies take time: the recommendations, especially of Royal Commissions, tend to disregard political considerations, and governments consequently view the results from a different angle than the public. Implementation thus takes even more time. To remit a problem to a Royal Commission in practice means putting off a decision for a considerable period: it is therefore sometimes used as a manoeuvre to avoid decisive action; the Canal Commission reported before the First World War: its recommendations were never put into practice. The Commons Commission was set up in 1955 and reported in 1958. Part of its recommendations became law in 1965.

Sometimes, however, the initiative comes from a different quarter, and the government is presented with a formulated problem or study by an unofficial body which may or may not have obtained civil service interest or help in the process. The responsible groups, conferences, seminars, or meetings come into existence usually because some problem is staring somebody in the face and he or she feels that something should be done. The compilation may be official, semi-official or unofficial; and sometimes no document is published at all but the event becomes important because of the quality of the participants and the effect of the discussions upon them and their contacts. The welfare of old people owes much to this sort of action by the National Council of Social Service; it was the National Federation of Women's Institutes which sponsored the campaign against litter; and the Duke of Edinburgh's 'Countryside in 1970' Conference has strongly influenced rural planning policy.

Lesser Government Offices

There are over a dozen offices which have no political head, which are of great practical importance but which function on their own under only the most sketchy parliamentary control. These include a cluster of institutions concerned with public finance such as the National Debt Office, the National Savings Committee, the Public Works Loans Commission and the Mint; valuable cheap legal services are provided for the public by the Public Trustee and the Land Registry; the Ordnance Survey with its maps, the London and Edinburgh Record Offices where enormous masses of documents are available for study, and the General Register Office with its population statistics provide much of the data needed for long-term planning. Lastly, there is the Friendly Societies Register and the increasingly important Charity Commission.

To these must be added that oddest of publishing undertakings Her Majesty's Stationery Office, which prints and publishes not only the huge and constantly changing flow of official documents and forms but sells miscellaneous things such as postcard reproductions of famous pictures and admirably produced guides to national monuments.

8

PARLIAMENT

Parliament is a corporation consisting of the Crown, the House of Lords and the House of Commons. The Crown alone can bring it into existence by summoning the Houses to meet; it comes automatically to an end after five years unless ended sooner by the exercise of the Crown's exclusive right of prorogation or dissolution. Prorogation ends a session and the same members can be summoned to a new session. Dissolution terminates the membership of the House of Commons and so a new parliament cannot be summoned until elections have been held to determine who the members shall be.

The House of Lords

Ceremonially there are ten categories of Lords who rank in a statutory order of precedence. For practical purposes these may be reduced to five: royal dukes who seldom appear except on ceremonial occasions; two archbishops and the bishops of London, Durham and Winchester who sit *ex officio* together with the twenty-one other senior bishops by date of appointment; Law Lords who are life members only and who sit mainly (but not exclusively) to strengthen the House as a supreme court of appeal; peers and peeresses appointed to hereditary or life peerages because of their personal distinction or political services; and peers and peeresses who have inherited their seats from an ancestor. The hereditary peers may be dukes, marquesses, earls, viscounts or barons or their feminine equivalents; all the life peers are barons or baronesses.

A peer, other than a peer of Ireland, who has no seat in the

House, cannot be a member of the House of Commons. An hereditary peerage may, however, be disclaimed for the life of the holder, in which case he can only return to the House of Lords as a life peer.

There is no legal limit to the size of the House which in April 1966 had 1,013 members. Of these 104 were life peers and 26 were bishops, but over two thirds of all peerages have been created since 1900. In practice only a small proportion of peers by inheritance actually attend, and those who do appear only when they have something to which they can make a special contribution. Except for a small daily allowance membership is unpaid.

Day to day business is carried on by the growing number of life peers and new creations. A peer cannot be unseated and so is free to speak his mind within the limits of political tact and ordinary decorum. The merits of great issues can therefore be discussed in the Lords without much fear of the party whips, and with considerable frankness and knowledge. The standard of debate has always been noticeably high.

The independence and permanence which a peerage confers makes it possible for peers to take up causes or represent organizations which otherwise might have no voice in Parliament; some, for instance, as chancellors of universities can act as the mouthpiece of academic opinion. One hereditary peer spoke only about white fish; and many national organizations, for instance for preserving rural amenities, for preventing cruelty, or for defending the rights of local authorities have, in effect, obtained a direct voice in the councils of the nation by securing the support of an interested peer. This has contributed greatly to the enrichment and balance of the governmental machine by ensuring that political parties and ministries do not have a monopoly of its workings. Moreover, the hereditary element has an advantage which could probably not be secured by any other means: a House of life peers if appointed for merit or eminence would in practice be an elderly body. Inheritance enables all ages as well as most interests to be represented.

On the other hand, the inevitably haphazard composition of the House makes it unreasonable for its powers to equal those of the Commons where the masses of the voters are represented; and in fact its powers are considerably less. It cannot prevent the passage of a money bill at all, and it can delay the passage of any other public bill by little more than a year. This gives it a decisive power only when a parliament is in its last year, that is to say when the last general election was several years ago and the state of the House of Commons might no longer accurately express the opinion of the country.

In comparison with the Commons the House of Lords as a legislative body has two peculiarities. It does not elect its own Speaker (or President) and it has very few standing orders. Its Speaker is the Lord Chancellor who as a senior Cabinet minister speaks in the House as a member of the government, and (partly for this reason) it manages its debates by agreement and not by direction from the chair. Peers consequently have to practise a restraint in speaking which is self-imposed; one who wishes to speak is expected to place his name on a list and indicate how long he thinks he will take: this involves detailed preparation of speeches and has a sobering effect on their quality.

The House also acts as a final court of appeal from courts in the United Kingdom. Theoretically any peer could sit; in practice only the so-called 'Law Lords', who are judges specially made life peers for the purpose, and peers who hold or have held high judicial office (such as the Lord Chancellor) ever take part. Until 1966 the House was considered to be bound by any precedents set by its own earlier judicial decisions; this rule was explicitly abandoned in July of that year so that the House can now, by way of appeal, pronounce that the law has changed.

62

The House of Commons

The country is divided into about 630 areas called constituencies whose boundaries are periodically rearranged by an independent commission. Within each of these every British subject of full age who has been resident there for about a year is entitled to be registered as a voter (elector) and if registered to vote. At a parliamentary election any number of qualified persons may stand as candidates provided that they can get ten people to sign their nomination papers and can deposit £150 with the Returning Officer who conducts the election. Election is by secret ballot and only one candidate can be elected to the House of Commons for each constituency, namely, the candidate who receives most votes. If there is a tie the Returning Officer draws lots between them. A candidate who receives less than one eighth of the votes cast forfeits his £150. The others get theirs back.

This electoral system has certain notable characteristics. The £150 deposit weights the scales against independents and small parties because large parties can maintain a pool of funds from which lost deposits can be made good. Secondly, it does not make certain that the opinion of the nation will be reflected in the composition of the House: in every contest where there are more than two reasonably well matched candidates it is, in fact, unlikely that the successful one will obtain more votes than the aggregate of his rivals and even where all the contests are 'straight' (i.e. with two candidates only) it is possible mathematically to envisage a situation where slightly over 25 per cent of the electors obtain a majority of one in the House. There have been several cases where a majority of the Commons was elected by a minority of the votes.

Thirdly, the system gives great influence to the comparatively small number of 'floating voters'. In general people vote according to their inclination, temperament, upbringing or inherited prejudice. This means that most people vote the same way at election after election. The balance within this huge mass of 'static voters' is therefore altered mainly by the appearance of new generations on the electoral roll and the death of old ones. There are, however, a number of electors who vote on the merits or believed merits of the issues which the election is likely to decide; though increasing, they are never numerous but they probably determine the country's future. A hypothetical example will make this clear: if in a straight contest 10,000 static voters will vote predictably for each candidate, the conscious decision of the one floating voter in an electorate of 20,001 will send one candidate or the other to Parliament. If the floating vote is 5 per cent of the total – a more probable event – and if there are three good candidates he who obtains 6,668 votes or more will be elected. The 1,000 floating voters will not all have voted the same way so that some of them will have cancelled each other out. The result in such a case can be – and often is – that about 3 per cent of the electors can secure the return to Parliament though 62 per cent voted for someone else.

Though the mathematical objections to this system are, in an egalitarian society, overwhelming, it is possible to justify it on the ground that it is precisely those who think about their vote who should influence the result. So long as they are in such a small minority this is probably reasonable, but it will break down if ever the floating voters become a majority.

The election being complete the House in due course meets on summons from the Crown; it elects a Speaker who is then presented to the Crown for approval (expressed in the House of Lords by the Lord Chancellor) and takes the chair. The House next adopts standing orders which in practice are the same from Parliament to Parliament and are very detailed; it is the Speaker's main business to rule the debates in accordance with these orders whose nature, especially in relation to procedure, is a very important part of the whole constitutional system.

The Speech from the Throne and General Policy

Before a new session of Parliament the Cabinet meets to settle its main policy and to set out in formal shape the measures which will be laid before the Houses to carry that policy out. Parliament meets only on summons from the Crown, and since parliaments began the Monarch has opened the proceedings in solemn session by declaring to the members 'the causes of the present Parliament being assembled'. This declaration is called the Speech from the Throne: and it is drafted for the Sovereign by the Cabinet at the meeting already mentioned. Not one word of it is nowadays the Sovereign's own. Sometimes it is delivered by Commissioners on his or her behalf, but in modern times it has almost always been delivered personally. This is the annual occasion known as the 'Opening of Parliament' and apart from the Coronation it is the most impressive ceremonial spectacle in the world. The peers in their robes wait in their places in the House of Lords: the Sovereign enters robed and crowned and is seated on the Throne. The Commons are summoned to the Bar headed by their Speaker. For a brief instant the ancient form of the medieval parliaments reappears like an illustration in an illuminated manuscript. The Lord Chancellor presents the speech on bended knee. The Sovereign reads it aloud, hands it back and retires, and the Houses then turn to their normal business.

Apart from the habitual first reading of a dummy bill to show their independence, the first business in each House is the discussion of a resolution to present an address of thanks to the Crown for the terms of the speech. This ceremonious form masks an operation of vast importance. The speech declares the policy of the government – of the party which has won the most recent general election – and if it cannot secure its vote of thanks in the House of Commons it will obviously be unable to persuade the House to support it in the detailed measures proposed. The debates last several days and provide opportunities for discussing and making

65

suggestions on every aspect of national policy. The occasion is the first test of confidence in the government which could not long survive a defeat 'on the address' in the Commons.

The recurrent if not quite annual* debates on the address are not the only times when resolutions not involving legislation are discussed, but they are the most important occasion when general policy comes under review. Resolutions on narrower issues will be considered at intervals throughout the session; some of these will be moved by the government, some by private members, some against the government by the organized opposition. They range from a non-committal invitation – say to 'take note' of a report of a commission – designed to provoke general reactions and suggestions, to a full-scale issue requiring an explanation of an aspect of policy and provoking reasoned and sometimes passionate attacks upon it. Probably the most important type of such a debate is a discussion on a white paper, that is to say a discussion of a document in which the government puts forward policy proposals on a particular subject such as the reorganization of the armed forces or the future of public transport. The points made in a white paper debate will often influence the form of legislation eventually based upon it.

Members' Freedom of Speech and Action

A member of either House may say anything he pleases, no matter how outrageous, within the House and in the course of its proceedings without fear that anyone will sue him for libel or slander. Anything which he says in these circumstances is said to be absolutely privileged and not amenable to any process in the courts. The privilege does not however extend beyond the walls of the House, and a slander or libel becomes actionable

---

* The Parliament which met in the spring of 1966 was adjourned, not prorogued, in August. There was no new session in the autumn and therefore no general parliamentary review of policy by debate on an address.

if he repeats it outside. A fair and accurate newspaper report of actual proceedings in a House has much the same protection as a member's speech.

It follows that the Houses have in the interests of intelligent and orderly debate to exert some control over the words of their members. They have an inherent right to ensure proper conduct and the ultimate modern sanction (very seldom used) in the Commons is expulsion and in the Lords 'refusal to hear further'. The basic principles are five; a member must not insult another member so as to create the probability of disorder; he must declare any personal interest which he may have in a subject under discussion; he must speak to the point; he must if challenged on a statement of fact either produce the evidence or withdraw; and when making a personal statement he must speak the truth.

Custom, and perhaps an exaggerated regard for the solidarity of governments also prescribes certain additional limitations on the now numerous holders of paid and unpaid offices. They are expected not to speak against the government's policy, and further, those who are paid are expected to stick to their ministerial specialization and are thus practically excluded from taking part in most debates and from sponsoring private members' bills.

Public Bills and Legislative Procedure

'Be it enacted by the Queen's Most Excellent Majesty by and with the advice and consent of the Lords Spiritual and Temporal and Commons in this present Parliament assembled and by the authority of the same as follows . . .'

This enacting formula (every word of which is important) expresses the nature of a statute more accurately than anything else can. There are circumstances – to be described later – where a bill can become an Act in ways other than those set out in the formula, but they are extremely rare. Now Parliament is a corporation created by summons and ended by prorogation or dissolution. Everything it does must be completed and effective before its end, otherwise it is nul. This rule is of fundamental practical importance for it requires every bill to pass *all* its stages from beginning to end in a single session – usually about a year; public business cannot ordinarily be held over from one session to another. Allowing for weekends, holidays, resolutions and committee business this has all kinds of effects of which the most important is that it severely limits the amount of legislation which can be passed. This will become more evident when considering the procedure to which all bills are submitted. The Time Factor is a vital element of the constitution and in choosing their legislative programme governments have to be much influenced by it alone. If there are several measures which a government wishes to pass it may simply because of this be forced to introduce them in successive sessions instead of simultaneously, and, of course, the passage of one bill may alter the circumstances of the next. It was to evade this fundamental principle that the Wilson government extended the first session of the new Parliament of 1966 by adjourning instead of proroguing the Houses.

In either House any member may introduce a bill and any so introduced are called public bills as opposed to private bills (see p. 73). Most public bills are brought in as part of government policy and are drafted in the ministries; private members' bills are sometimes privately drafted, but are quite often drawn up with the help of government draftsmen; a decision to allow such a draftsman to be used for this purpose is a clear indication (generally construed as an undertaking) that the government will support the bill.

Except for bills involving taxation or expenditure from public funds any bill may be introduced into either House where it will be read a first time. These 'readings' used to take place in the days when not all members were literate, but nowadays an order for a reading is simply an order to move to the next stage. The first reading is formal and automatic and is really the method of giving notice of what is afoot; usually the bill has not even been drafted.

Once drafted it is printed and published and is then considered on second reading, when its general purposes and principles are in issue. Every bill has its first and second readings in the House in which it originated. Most second reading debates are held by the whole House but recently the House of Commons has introduced a second reading committee to which a bill can be referred unless twenty members object. Obviously this is likely to affect only minor bills.

If the general purpose and principles of a bill are approved, it is sent to a committee to be considered word by word and amended if necessary in detail. The committee may consist of all the members of the House and in the Lords it often does; in the Commons, on the other hand, almost every bill is considered in one of the standing committees (each of about sixty members), and a committee stage 'on the floor of the House' now happens less than once in a session. Thus at a busy time of the year as many as six Commons committees may be considering legislation simultaneously in the mornings.

When the committee stage is finished the results are reported to the House which then has a further opportunity to make detailed amendments, after which it is debated again as amended on the third reading.

The bill then goes to the other House where it receives much the same treatment. If it remains unaltered it is then ready for assent by the Sovereign. If it has been rejected by the second House that is the end of it, unless the second House is the House of Lords and the government is determined to 'use the Parliament Acts'. If, which is commonly the case, the second House amends it, the amendments must be agreed by the first House before it can receive the royal assent.

A money bill, that is a bill imposing a tax or granting funds to the Treasury, must be introduced into the House of Commons which is therefore always the first House, and though the Lords may debate it, they cannot prevent its being presented for the royal assent beyond one month after they have received it from the Commons. To apply this rule strictly a bill must be certified to be a money bill by the Speaker of the House of Commons; there are many bills which contain money clauses but which are mostly concerned with other things; such bills are sometimes introduced into the Lords, who pass them without the money clauses and leave the Commons to put them in, or they are sent up from the Commons without a Speaker's Certificate so that non-money clauses can be properly considered.

Money bills also have a further and important peculiarity. Before they can be sent to committee in the House of Commons a resolution permitting the necessary imposition or expenditure must be passed in committee of the whole House. This resolution must be moved on behalf of the Crown or with its assent: a private member can move a reduction of a tax or expenditure but cannot move an increase. This is a very important constitutional rule which in effect transfers the initiation of new taxation and expenditure outside Parliament and into the field of negotiation.

In the event of major disagreement between the Houses there are two ways in which eventually the Commons can impose their will. The oldest and most drastic method is for the Prime Minister to advise the Sovereign to create enough peers to ensure a government majority in the Lords. This actually happened in 1712 when twelve new peerages were created, and the threat was successfully used in 1832 and 1910. The more modern method is that of the Parliament Acts whereby, if the Lords reject a public bill and the same bill without alteration is sent to them again in the next session a year later it may be presented for the Royal Assent over their heads. This method has been used only three times since 1911.*

A bill must, thus, go through at least eleven and sometimes as many as fifteen stages before it can be presented for the royal

---

* The period was three sessions and two years under the Act of 1911 but was reduced in 1949. The 'rule of 1949' has not yet been used.

assent. Each of these needs time and between each there must be an interval. By itself this is a formidable matter and goes a long way towards explaining why time is so important in Parliament: but there is another factor which is the yearly timetable itself. Parliaments normally meet in November, the Budget is usually in April and the session ends (apart from a few cleaning up days in October) at the end of July. The budget is followed by many days throughout the summer when the Commons are engaged on the estimates of the ministries – the so-called Supply Days. This is the time when individual ministerial policy is being considered and criticized, and the House is apt to be preoccupied. Hence it follows that hardly any bill introduced after March has much chance of success unless the government will help or steam-roller it through.

This severely curtails the legislative opportunities of the private member. The amount of parliamentary time pre-empted by government policy and financial debate is so great that the remainder is quite insufficient for private members to turn all their many good ideas into law or even to get them debated. If twenty-five private members' bills are introduced in a session it is improbable that more than eight will pass. This has driven the Commons into the unfortunate expedient of the private members' ballot: participants names are drawn at random and the first twenty or so are given an opportunity to introduce a bill. Those six or eight who obtain an early date for a second reading have a fair future. The rest usually fall by the wayside – but are sometimes picked up again in another session.

The rigour of this situation is slightly mitigated by the so-called ten-minute rule: a member can seek leave to introduce a bill by a ten-minute speech to which a ten-minute reply is allowed. The House then divides on the first reading. In view of the many later hurdles, it is obvious that the content of such a bill must be uncontroversial (and probably unimportant) to have any chance.

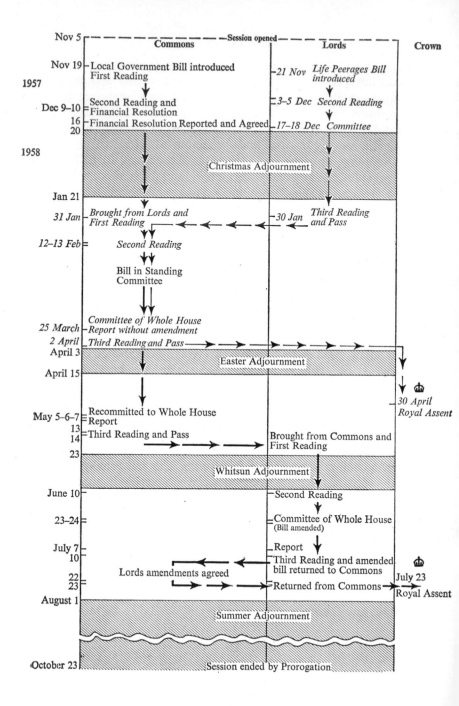

Nov 5 ‒ ‒ ‒ ‒ ‒ ‒ ‒ ‒ ‒ ‒ Session opened ‒ ‒ ‒ ‒ ‒ ‒ ‒

Commons **Lords** **Crown**

Nov 19 ‒ Local Government Bill introduced
First Reading
‒21 Nov *Life Peerages Bill
introduced*

1957

Dec 9–10 ‒ Second Reading and
Financial Resolution
‒3–5 Dec *Second Reading*

16 ‒ Financial Resolution Reported and Agreed
20
17–18 Dec Committee

1958

Christmas Adjournment

Jan 21

31 Jan *Brought from Lords and
First Reading*
‒30 Jan *Third Reading
and Pass*

12–13 Feb ‒ *Second Reading*

Bill in Standing
Committee

Committee of Whole House
25 March ‒ Report without amendment

2 April ‒ *Third Reading and Pass* →→→→→→→→→
April 3

Easter Adjournment

April 15

♚
30 April
Royal Assent

Recommitted to Whole House
May 5–6–7 ‒ Report
13 ‒ Third Reading and Pass
14 → → → → → Brought from Commons and
First Reading
23

Whitsun Adjournment

June 10 ‒ Second Reading

23–24 ‒ Committee of Whole House
(Bill amended)

July 7 ‒ Report
10 ‒ Third Reading and amended
bill returned to Commons

♚
July 23
Royal Assent

22 ‒ Lords amendments agreed ← ← ←
23 ‒ → → → → Returned from Commons
August 1

Summer Adjournment

October 23 Session ended by Prorogation

Private Bills

The right of petition is an ancient liberty, and it is possible for persons not in either House to introduce into Parliament by means of a petition a private bill dealing with some interest or direct concern of their own. This must be done if at all on one day at the end of November in each year. A draft bill accompanies the petition and this must contain a preamble justifying the provisions in the bill itself. The proceedings on private bills are the same as those on public bills except that certain notices must be published and served on various interested people, and that at the committee stage a very small committee hears evidence for and against the preamble and clauses, much as a case is tried in court: indeed, barristers appear for the interested parties. If the preamble cannot be proved the whole bill is rejected.

Bills of this sort are more significant and frequent than is commonly realised; upwards of twenty are passed every year. Parliament, indeed, publishes a book of model clauses for such bills so as to standardize them as much as possible. The railways, waterways, harbours and the gas and electricity industries are managed mainly under private acts, and most county and county borough councils have private acts and even whole codes of them. They are an important feature of local administration.

Fig. 6. THE PROGRESS OF LEGISLATION
The chart shows the 1957/8 Session of Parliament and the progress of the Local Government and the Life Peerages Bills. The Local Government Bill involved expenditure and had to commence in the Commons, where the committee stage was (unusually) taken both in standing committee and on the floor of the House. It was heavily amended. The Life Peerages Bill involved no expenditure and was commenced in the Lords. Owing to its constitutional importance the committee stages in both Houses were taken on the floor. The bill was not amended.

The Royal Assent

No bill can become law without the Royal Assent. It may come into force, once it has received it, at any time laid down in its provisions, but if no such time is laid down it comes into force when the assent is given. Contrary to a common belief a bill is not signed by the Sovereign. The assent is given by word of mouth in the House of Lords: the words could be spoken for the Sovereign in person, but actually the assent is given by Commissioners who are specifically authorized to assent in the Sovereign's name to particular bills set out in their commission. This authorizing document *is* signed by the Sovereign.

The assent is in fact spoken by the Clerk of the Parliaments in Norman French.*

The Relative Functions of the Two Houses

In every year a great many legislative changes are proposed. Some are of political importance or for one reason or another engage the passions of the public, and it is natural that on these issues action should be commenced in the House of Commons where the people are represented, and that the Commons should have their way.

On the other hand, there are many proposals which, though important, are technical rather than political – a bill, for instance, to codify a branch of law or to simplify the regulation of taxicabs – and provided that the rules on money bills permit, it is more sensible that this sort of proposal should be considered first in the cooler and more detached atmosphere of the House of Lords. Moreover, every bill has its technical aspect and this can equally well be regularized in the Upper House. Thus

---

* For a bill granting money to the Crown the formula of assent is 'La Reyne remercie ses bons sujets, accepte leur benevolence, et ainsi le veult.' For other public and local bills it is, 'La Reyne le veult', and for personal bills 'Soit fait comme il est desiree'. Assent was last refused in 1707; the formula for refusal would be 'La Reyne s'avisera.' A new alternative method of giving the assent through the Lord Chancellor is proposed.

one House enforces the will of the electors, while the other makes the opinions of experts public.

This arrangement in two Houses is very convenient; for it makes it possible to have two queues of bills – the one technical, the other popular – moving simultaneously through Parliament in opposite directions. If there were only one House every sort of bill would have to move in the same direction and all bills would be in the same queue. In practice this would lead to one of two results; either technical legislation would never pass, or the only House would subdivide into committees of such power that the control of the House as a whole might be lost.

Relationships between the Houses and Ministries

Apart from issues which arise in discussions on the address, on White Papers and on bills, the conduct of individual ministries passes under scrutiny in both Houses through three principal types of proceedings. In the first place the estimates of all the Ministries come up annually for discussion in the Commons between (roughly) Easter and August. This is the time when members who specialize in some branch of public affairs have opportunities to criticize and offer constructive suggestions for the administration of particular aspects of the nation's life.

Secondly, about an hour is allotted every day in the House of Commons to enable members to question ministers about matters within their competence. Notice of a question is given in advance and when the reply has been given oral supplementary questions are allowed. There is no rule of law that requires a question to be answered, and replies are sometimes in fact refused, but for obvious political reasons (including the risk of an adjournment debate) Ministers are ready to answer the great majority. Question time in the Commons is usually a lively, not to say entertaining, episode.

This simplified account of question time is in fact too simple.

75

Many questions are put down solely to obtain uncontroversial information and the answer is requested and given in writing; so that more is elicited than at first appears. On the other hand so many questions are put down for oral answer that it is never possible to reply to all or even most of them. There is one other important feature of parliamentary questions: they take priority in the business of the ministry to which they are addressed and therefore interrupt the normal work of civil servants, who, being human may be understandably irritated; it follows that a parliamentary question is not always the best way of securing a favourable ministerial decision.

The third form of control is through the medium of the adjournment debate. Any member can move the adjournment of the House or resist the routine adjournment on the ground that public grievances yet remain undiscussed. Adjournment debates may arise out of any public event or even an unsatisfactory answer to a question. The practical effect of carrying the point would be to interfere with the government's parliamentary timetable and so indirectly with the Cabinet's general policy; it is therefore a method of bringing pressure upon a ministry through the Cabinet.

The Uses of Ceremonial

A distinguishing feature of the British parliament is its procedural ceremonial. This is now under fashionable but wrongheaded attack. Something is needed to mark off one stage of a parliamentary process from another and a ceremony (if not prolonged) will do as well as anything else; archaism is a positive advantage as a regular reminder that those present are only a link in a continuing process; but especially ceremony is a form of discipline compelling members to behave with dignity, and dignity is nowhere more important than in the conduct of national affairs, The few minutes a day spent in ceremonial could not be much better used.

Part Three

INSTRUMENTS OF GOVERNMENT

9

SUBLEGISLATION

Because Parliament can do anything, it can and frequently does confer upon others power to make sub-laws. This power is ordinarily limited fairly strictly by the enabling Act and its exercise in a particular case can often be challenged in the courts: someone who thinks that a sub-law is illegal may disobey it and meet any charge brought against him with the defence that he is not bound by it. There is no other direct method of attacking the legality of sub-laws except in Parliament, with the result that it can happen that the public obeys a rule for years because no one has thought of risking prosecution.

The term 'sub-law' is not a term of art, but embraces all types of rules made by someone who is not Parliament. The powers, already mentioned, of the legislatures in Northern Ireland and the island dependencies are high examples of this function; another is the power of the Assembly of the Church of England to pass Measures. The Sovereign makes many Orders in Council, and ministers can make orders or regulations on matters relating to their respective departments; the subject matter ranges from the trivial to the vital: for instance the Lord Chancellor can prescribe what corporations may act as Custodian Trustees, the Minister concerned with local government makes orders for the distribution of millions in grants, and the Minister of Transport can prescribe the shape, type and size of road signs. Most of these general orders, rules and regulations are embodied in so-called statutory instruments distinguished by a name, year and number and published in a continuous series. More than 2,000 are made every year.

Constitutionally they can be distinguished into three sorts: those made without recourse to Parliament, those which are laid before the Houses and come into force after forty days if neither House rejects them, and those which require positive affirmation by each House. The two latter methods of parliamentary control are in some ways defective. There are too many orders for proper scrutiny and Parliament can only accept or reject an order as a whole: it cannot amend it. The chances of rejection because of objections of detail are slight for obvious reasons, and so orders with objectionable features can be 'steam-rollered' through Parliament. In real life ministries try to prevent this by consulting those likely to be affected: this is a matter of general interest because the method of regulation by order is convenient and its abuse could lead to great difficulties if Parliament became suspicious of the method. It should be added that Ministers do not exhaust the category of sublegislators under parliamentary control: other important institutions such as the Rules Committee of the Supreme Court are in the same position.

Besides the central authorities there are many local bodies such as county councils with similar powers, limited to their areas and competence. The sub-laws made by them are called by-laws and they require confirmation by a Minister: in England he is nearly always the Home Secretary; in Scotland and Wales the relevant Secretary of State. By-laws mostly deal with minor matters such as behaviour in parks, and are enforced by small fines. As they make a local addition to the law which strangers cannot be expected to know, the Home Office or other department is reluctant to confirm by-laws and encourages authorities to base them on its own published model drafts*.

* There are several series of these model draft by-laws dealing with different classes of subjects. They can be purchased at H.M. Stationery Office.

10

COURTS AND INQUIRIES

The activities of thousands of companies and businesses, not to mention those of 56,000,000 people each acting in many different capacities, make collisions and disputes inevitable. These may occur between individuals or between an individual and the 'State' (i.e. the general body of citizens); the subject matter of a dispute may be whether one side has a 'right' or whether (in a dispute with the State) an individual is 'wrong', or whether some administrative act should or should not be performed. Modern society is immensely complex with its garage hands and actors, policemen and clergy, seamen, inventors, programmers, farmers and so forth. A complicated situation cannot be run by simple rules, for simple rules would seldom fit a real life situation. For this reason a short description of the ways in which disputes are settled can only be very rough.

Three procedures and institutions can be distinguished. There are civil procedures and courts, criminal procedures and courts and a whole host of people and bodies empowered to deal with administrative arguments: these latter will here be called *inquiries*. The essential difference between a court and an inquiry is that a court must decide an issue in accordance with law whereas an inquiry sits to discover facts which will enable someone, not necessarily itself, to make an administrative decision. If I find Jones in my house the civil court will determine whether he has any right to it and if not it will eject him; if I am accused of stealing, the criminal court will establish whether or not I am guilty and will punish or release me in accordance with its finding. But if I wish to convert my house into a restaurant and the planning authority refuses me permission, the resulting inquiry, when I appeal to the Minister, collects facts which will enable him to make the most convenient decision in all the circumstances. Courts deal with rights and wrongs, inquiries with policy.

Unfortunately this distinction is not always easy to follow in a particular case. In an inquiry there may be a bitter dispute between private citizens so that the proceedings seem like a trial in court: a houseowner may wish to protect his family life by preventing the establishment of a factory next door, but the business man who wants to open the factory may depend upon it for his and his family's living. In such a case the inquiry takes on the appearance of a straight fight in court, but actually the Minister will eventually have to decide something quite different – namely whether in the interest of the locality (and sometimes the nation) it is a good thing to place a factory on that site.

Courts

The chart in Fig. 7 is divided horizontally between overseas and United Kingdom and vertically between civil and criminal. Only the English judicial system is shown in detail; the Northern Irish system resembles it, the Scottish is noticeably different though the distinction between civil and criminal is still valid.

At the bottom are the petty sessional courts staffed in the big cities by single paid ('stipendiary') magistrates, who are professional lawyers but elsewhere by at least two lay Justices of the Peace (J.P.s) helped by a professional clerk. Of their business 80 per cent is petty crime and motoring offences, but they also deal with matrimonial disputes and a few administrative ones. There is a right of appeal from a magistrates' court; if it is on a point of law it goes to the High Court; if on a point of fact there is a rehearing before the justices at Quarter Sessions.

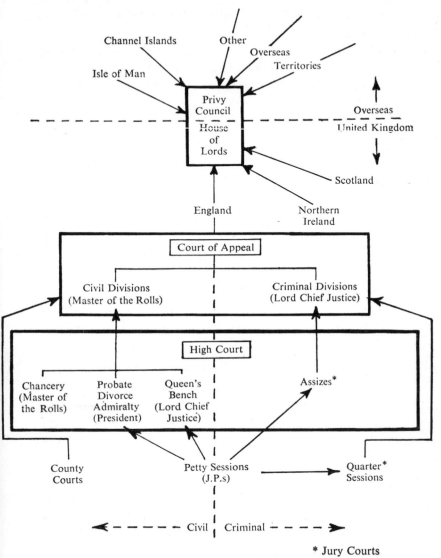

Fig. 7. THE LEGAL SYSTEM

* Jury Courts

Serious charges are tried by a jury at Quarter Sessions where a professional lawyer presides, and very serious charges at Assizes which are held before a High Court Judge. In either case the defendant can appeal on a point of law to the Criminal Division of the Court of Appeal. From this court there is a right of Appeal to the House of Lords only in capital cases and in cases certified by the Attorney General as involving a point of great public importance.

On the civil side smaller disputes are heard in the County Court and the rest in one of the divisions of the High Court. Matters concerning wills, marriages and shipping go before the Probate Divorce and Admiralty Division because these three branches of our law are derived from Roman law. The Chancery Division deals with property, family settlements, trusts and the guardianship of children. Other disputes such as breaches of contract, libel, negligence, assault and battery, intimidation and so forth are the domain of the Queen's Bench.

Civil appeals on a point of law go first to the Court of Appeal and finally to the House of Lords.

Appointments, Status and Protection of Judicial Officers

Judges of the High Court and Court of Appeal must have been practising barristers and are appointed by the Sovereign on the recommendation of the Lord Chancellor. They retire at seventy-five, and can be dismissed only if both Houses of Parliament petition the Crown for dismissal. This has never yet happened. Their salaries are high and are charged on the consolidated fund and are therefore paid automatically without annual consideration by the House of Commons. When travelling on circuit judges are required to use official residences and given travelling staffs. In these ways they are protected, so far as is humanly possible, from any form of official or private pressure. Judicial Members of the House of Lords, being peers, cannot be unseated at all.

84

County court judges are also barristers and so, generally, are the stipendiary magistrates who function in the larger cities. They are appointed by the Lord Chancellor and can only be dismissed with such difficulty that they invariably last until retirement at seventy-two. Their salaries are almost as secure as the High Court Judges.

Justices of the Peace are laymen appointed by the Lord Chancellor on the recommendation of the Lord Lieutenant and a committee in each county. They are unpaid but numerous and they seldom sit alone.

Methods of Trial

Trial procedure is based on the principle that matters of law must be decided by the legal expert – the Judge – but that questions of fact must be decided by the same sort of people as the parties themselves, that is by laymen; in England twelve of whom sit together as a jury who must be unanimous*. The jury is chosen at random from the public by lot, which makes it difficult to know in advance who they will be and minimizes the risk of corruption; their opinion (called their 'verdict') is conclusive on the facts as long as it is based on admissible evidence; and in a criminal trial a verdict of 'Not Guilty' is final.

The conclusive nature of a verdict on the facts is one reason why appeals are possible only on questions of law; but it is also the theoretical keystone of the fairness of justice, for it brings the common sense of the ordinary man into a vital (not a minor) part of the trial, and an accused is protected against oppression by the power of his twelve equals on the jury to release him whatever *anyone* says. Jury trial is more than that: it is a safeguard against bad laws passed by a parliament out of touch with the public because if ever such laws were made juries would refuse to convict under them. In the days when

* This was written before proposals for majority verdicts were introduced into the House of Commons. The author believes that there is much danger and little justification for this change.

death was the penalty for a long list of comparatively minor offences they often did so.

The efficiency of jury trial depends upon the judge ensuring that the jury hears and sees only such evidence as can fairly be placed before them for the purpose of deciding the question at issue. For instance it is fair to bring an eyewitness forward because the value of his evidence can be tested by cross-questioning; it is not fair to bring someone forward to say what someone else (not in court) saw, because the truth can only be tested by questioning that someone else. The law of procedure upon which fairness and therefore liberty depend is mostly a series of rules on what should and what should not be placed before a jury, and when there is a dispute on such a question the jury is sent out while the matter is argued.

Now it might be thought from the foregoing that trial by jury would be common and indeed normal. Unfortunately this is not so. In civil cases other than defamation and breach of promise it is now so rare that it can almost be said to have been abolished, and over 90 per cent of criminal matters are heard before magistrates (who are not 'ordinary' people) alone. In other words our celebrated jury system only operates in 3 per cent of cases at most.

This is a matter of serious criticism. The procedure is designed to separate the trial of facts and of law. If there is no jury the same person must try both; a moment comes when he must decide whether certain evidence is admissible – whether, that is to say, a jury could be permitted to hear it if a jury were there. If he decides to admit, all is well; if he decides to exclude, the exclusion is from his own mind which is necessarily seized of the matter. This exercise in intellectual self-control is doubtless performed successfully quite often, mainly by professionals – but in practice it has to be performed thousands of times a week by lay magistrates. It is hard to be sure that justice is reliably based on so difficult a foundation, and, in addition, it dissociates the public from participation in the course of justice.

Inquiries

There are over 2,000 bodies and tribunals which hold inquiries to discover facts leading, as already explained, not to logical conclusions, but to policy decisions. Their variety is inexhaustible. A parliamentary inquiry has been held into the alleged relationship between a minister and a spy. The Board of Trade can investigate the affairs of a company. Wreck Commissioners investigate accidents at sea. Military courts inquire into alleged desertions. Ministry of Labour inquiries are held into strikes, and inspectors of the Ministry of Housing and Local Government investigate objections to boundary changes and planning appeals.

Most such inquiries have certain features in common; they are held to assemble facts on a special question and so are appointed temporarily. The Minister or other appointing body is entitled to obtain information by other means though generally he must give notice to those involved if he does. The inquiry is held in public, usually by a civil servant who is often a specialist in holding such inquiries; there is no set procedure, though witnesses are commonly examined and cross-examined in the manner of a trial at law. Depending on the nature of the event, there may be a great many people who wish to be heard so that a major inquiry, such as that on the reorganization of local authorities in the West Midlands, can go on for weeks. At the end no 'judgement' is given, but the inspector makes a written report and recommendations to his Minister and sends copies to the interested parties. If the Minister decides otherwise than in accordance with the inspector's views he must usually state his reasons for so doing.

The general conduct of inquiries is kept under supervision by the Council on Tribunals to whom complaints can be made. The Council is not, however, a court of appeal; it is really a standing public inquiry into public inquiries, and makes recommendations on their conduct to ministers and to Parliament.

Special Tribunals and Domestic Courts

A description of our public institutions would be incomplete without mention of a type of tribunal whose functions fall somewhere between a law court and an inquiry. Such tribunals are permanent, but deal with a special problem such as housing, rents, or disability pensions. They are created by law and controlled by the High Court solely to ensure that they conduct their business fairly and do not overstep the limits of their jurisdiction.

Side by side with these official tribunals are the disciplinary committees or 'domestic courts' of the more important public professions such as medicine, law, pilotage and so forth. These control the standard of professional ethics of their members by the exercise of a right to expel a practitioner and so deprive him of his livelihood. Their proper functioning is of public importance because on the one hand they can inflict an enormous effective penalty, while on the other the body politic cannot do without the type of professional person whom they control. For this reason their activities are under a jurisdiction of the High Court which is very similar to that which it exercises over the special tribunals.

11

PUBLIC REVENUES

Enormous sums are needed to carry on public business. In 1966–7 the Government expenditure was expected to be £9,177 millions and local authority expenditure £1,430 millions in addition. To this must be added the operations of national industries and government undertakings and the income of charities. The money has to come from somewhere: Fig. 8 sets out the major (but not all) the kinds or sources of public revenue.

Charities

A charity is a fund set up for a public purpose but privately administered. There are five main types of charity namely, education, relief of poverty, religion, public recreation and miscellaneous purposes such as the relief of sickness and the repair of bridges. As the objects of legal charity are matters which would otherwise have to be met from public funds, charitable income is not taxable. On the other hand, to ensure that the funds really are applied properly, all charities have to be registered and are supervised by the Charity Commissioners* and ultimately by the Attorney General and the High Court.

The number of charities is gigantic and constantly growing and they vary greatly in purpose and endowments. There are ancient widows' charities worth no more than a few pounds a year, and bodies such as the Nuffield Foundation worth tens of millions. They include universities and colleges and public

* Or the Department of Education and Science in the case of an educational fund.

bodies like the National Council of Social Service, and the Royal National Lifeboat Institution. Their importance is very great; their collective wealth is considerable, and because they enable people to give public service without being involved with politics or official institutions of any sort, and without being officials themselves, and because they can back new ideas with money in a way which officialdom cannot, they exert a leverage quite disproportionate to their apparent weight.

Taxes and Rates

A tax is any impost payable to the government. The rates are a particular form of impost payable only to local authorities.

All taxes are at some stage paid over to a tax collector, but it is convenient to classify them as 'direct' or 'indirect' according to whether the taxpayer himself bears the burden directly or whether he is in a position indirectly to impose it on someone else by adding to the price of something which he sells.

The principal direct taxes are the capital taxes such as the so-called death duties and the capital gains taxes, and the taxes on income called 'income tax', surtax and corporation tax. Income tax and surtax are levied on personal income and earnings at amounts which vary according to income and family circumstances. Profits tax is levied at a flat rate on company earnings; many companies, however, carry on international business and have installations abroad. To prevent the entire profits of international trade being swallowed up in national taxation, governments make so-called double taxation agreements; the commonest principle of these is that a company pays no more in total taxation than the higher rate levied in the two countries concerned, and the two countries then divide the proceeds in accordance with a formula.

Of the main indirect taxes, customs are levied at ports

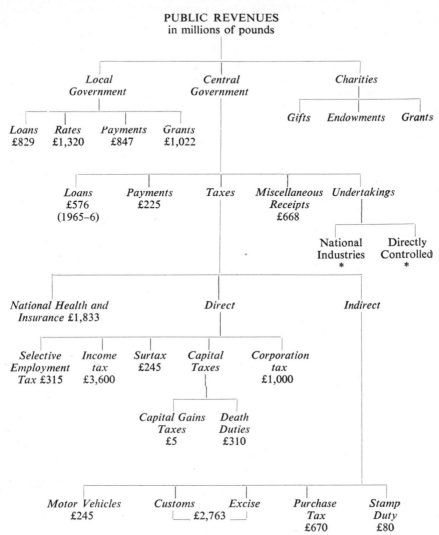

PUBLIC REVENUES
in millions of pounds

Local Government

Loans	Rates	Payments	Grants
£829	£1,320	£847	£1,022

Central Government

Loans £576 (1965–6)	Payments £225	Taxes	Miscellaneous Receipts £668	Undertakings

Undertakings: National Industries *   Directly Controlled *

Taxes: National Health and Insurance £1,833 — Direct — Indirect

Direct

Selective Employment Tax £315	Income tax £3,600	Surtax £245	Capital Taxes	Corporation tax £1,000

Capital Taxes: Capital Gains Taxes £5 — Death Duties £310

Indirect

Motor Vehicles £245	Customs	Excise	Purchase Tax £670	Stamp Duty £80

£2,763 (Customs and Excise)

Charities: Gifts   Endowments   Grants

* Revenue absorbed by the undertakings themselves.

Fig. 8. PUBLIC REVENUES

Figures for 1966 except local government (1965–66)

91

and aerodromes on imported goods, and excise duties on goods manufactured internally. The beer duty is an excise. In addition purchase taxes are levied on a wide range of goods of both foreign and home origin; there are, as a result, cases where more than one of these imposts is payable on the same article.

Lastly, there are miscellaneous imposts such as pools and betting duty, and the stamp duties. The most familiar of the latter are the stamps on cheques and contracts, but there are some substantial stamp duties charged as a percentage of the amount involved on sales of shares and land, and on deeds of covenant.

Payments and Directly Controlled Undertakings

Both the government and the local authorities have properties (such as houses) for which they receive large amounts mostly by way of rent. There are also undertakings such as the Royal Mint which execute contracts for other bodies (including foreign governments) and also from time to time sales of public property – such as surplus war stores after the Second World War – realize considerable sums. These sources of revenue are erratic, but in the aggregate they are important.

The Post Office used to be a leading revenue-producing undertaking, but it is now treated as if it were a firm and makes payments to the Treasury as if it were taxable. H.M. Stationery Office, on the other hand, makes a consistent loss because though it is one of the largest publishers in the world it has to bear the burden of much unsaleable government printing.

Operations of National Industries

The national industries each keep separate accounts so that their expenditure has to be set against revenue to arrive at a true or net result. In fact their respective finances differ very widely; there seldom is a surplus which can be handed over to the Treasury and, on the contrary, the Treasury has sometimes to come to their rescue.

Public surface transport, especially the railways, has always made a loss. Efforts to correct the balance by reducing rail mileage and service to the public have so far understandably failed, but the responsible boards have been permitted to write off losses.

Atomic energy presents a converse picture. Here the present revenue is small but losses, which are very large, represent capital investment intended to make the kingdom a country of the atomic age. The expenditures of the Authority are savings from which a benefit should be reaped later on.

Between the extremes of shrinkage and expansion lie gas and electricity; though they do from time to time borrow they are required as far as possible to finance their capital development from revenue. They therefore charge in order to produce an annual surplus, and plough the proceeds back into the business. They have made notable progress as is proved by the advancing high-tension grids, and the revolution in importing and producing town gas.

The coal industry is dominated by the peculiar life-cycle of a coal-mine: it begins in a small way, requires capital to bring it to a high level of production, employs at that time much specialized labour which has to be locally resident and is very self-conscious, and then slowly declines as the seams are worked out. Coal-mine management involves social problems: there is a pressure to keep a mine going for the sake of families, and a social as well as financial incentive to keep the labour force small from the start by a massive use of machinery. Governments are sometimes tempted to intervene on social pretexts: the demand for coal is falling steadily as it is more efficiently used. To prevent unemployment the gas and electricity industries improvement schemes (which involve a movement away from coal) are sometimes delayed. The disadvantage to the rest of the public may, perhaps, be considered a hidden addition to the cost of unemployment benefit.

Loans

Local Authorities borrow almost exclusively for capital works, but the government borrows for all sorts of purposes (including wars) depending on the general economic situation. The total of public borrowing is very large, and broadly speaking takes three forms – loans of indefinite duration, loans repayable after some years at a fixed date, and Treasury Bills.

Loans of indefinite duration such as $2\frac{1}{2}$ per cent 'Consols' are not repayable by the government except at its own option. The lender is in effect buying a perpetual right to interest on the money which he has paid, but this right is saleable. Obviously the usefulness of this method of borrowing depends on the existence of a market where such rights can easily be dealt in: the stock exchanges are in fact such a market and so play a very significant part in government finance.

The so-called 'dated stocks' are loans repayable at a time which may be between three and as much as forty years after the original borrowing. There are always a large number of these stocks outstanding at any time and they, like undated stocks, are dealt in on the stock exchanges. Nowadays when the date for repayment comes it is common for the government to raise a new loan and repay part or most of the old one out of the proceeds.

Compared with government stocks Treasury Bills are of a different order and much more resemble temporary overdrafts. Expenditure and revenue do not march in step and there are moments during a year when more money is needed than has become available to the Treasury through ordinary channels. Accordingly, Treasury Bills repayable in full in three months' time are offered to banks at a small discount, in theory to tide over these difficult intervals. The turnover of these bills is large and in fact they are used from time to time as a means of raising bigger sums than the immediate situation requires. This, of course, puts off the need to raise another long term loan on the market, but sometimes results in Treasury Bills being used to repay Treasury Bills; there is accordingly a substantial so-called 'floating debt'.

12

NATIONAL INDUSTRIES AND CONTROLLED PROFESSIONS

There are corporations which have trading functions but which are really part of the government apparatus. These include the Industrial Reorganization Corporation, the Forestry Commission, two airways corporations, 'Cable and Wireless', the Atomic Energy Authority, the Colonial Development Corporation, two organizations concerned with fish, one with sugar and one with iron and steel. A controversial feature of the management of the country is the position of these and of four other important industries which are no longer run for profit but supply goods or services to the public. The four other industries are coal-mining, gas, electricity and public transport. The Post Office is in fact the oldest such industry.

The motives which led to the present situation were in each case somewhat different. Thus the idea that power in all its forms should be in public ownership is logically a justification for taking coal, gas and electricity out of private hands, but actually the leading motive in the case of coal was to improve the lot of the coal-miners, while some gas and electrical undertakings had been in municipal hands long before their ownership and management was centralized.

The Post Office apart, the nationalized industries are in a peculiar and not wholly satisfactory constitutional position. They own tremendous assets, they employ hundreds of thousands and their annual operations run into hundreds of millions of pounds. Without them the country would come to a standstill in a few days. They are a vital part of the way in which the kingdom is governed and some of their managements exert as much influence as any government department, yet they are run not by ministers responsible to Parliament but by boards appointed by ministers. The importance of this distinction is much greater than at first appears: the boards are responsible for day to day management and indeed for much of the policy; the Minister only comes in on matters of the very highest national importance. It follows that he can be attacked in Parliament only on high policy; and an aggrieved individual, whose difficulty is not often at so imposing a level, can seldom obtain the help of his M.P. about his problem.

But the boards of the four great industries operate a total monopoly within their special field so that the dissatisfied customer cannot go to a trade rival. To soften these difficulties the framers of the transport, gas and electricity nationalization acts resorted to the device of the Consultative Council, which is appointed (like the board) by the appropriate Minister from organizations which he considers have an interest in the efficiency of the industry. The Councils, as their name implies, have no executive function and cannot compel the managements to do anything, and moreover their secretariats are provided by their managements. Their value is thus limited to that which they can achieve by their influence as people and by their ability to express the views of consumers acceptably. The usefulness of these weak institutions has varied greatly and not all of them have achieved the complete confidence of the public.

Besides these government-owned or financed organizations there are several bodies connected with trades or professions whose activities are enforceable by law. Amongst these are marketing boards for such commodities as milk and eggs, and the governing bodies of the legal and medical professions which have power to admit to membership and can therefore control standards of competence. Both types of organization have two purposes in common: the maintenance of a reasonable living by those with whom they are concerned, and the maintenance of proper standards for the benefit of the public.

13

LOCAL ADMINISTRATION

Despite local variations mentioned in the first chapter, the government of the kingdom is exceedingly centralized and tending to become more so. In this chapter it is proposed to summarize the way in which administration is carried out locally. This is not, as in France, based upon a standardized or even a rational pattern but, as with other things, has been the effect of historical accidents. The result is sometimes inconvenient.

Local administration is carried on through five main types of organization: these are the local organs of certain ministries, the sub-managements of nationalized industries, specialist authorities, the so-called local authorities which are sometimes collectively but not very happily called 'Local Government' and finally the Regional Bodies. Each type uses a pattern and geographical layout to suit itself and regardless of the rest so that areas and jurisdictions overlap four, five, six and even ten-fold.

Local Offices of Ministries

It is inevitable that specialist ministries such as the armed services should have local outstations. An army without local units would hardly be an army; and there are several other ministries which control great local interests through their own provincial offices. For instance, the huge sums involved in pensions and national insurance are mostly handled in this way. The Ministry of Agriculture has a powerful network of committees concerned with the efficiency of farming; the hospitals are managed through Regional Hospital Boards of the Ministry of Health, and the valuation of properties (which is important both to national and to local finance) is carried out by staffs controlled by the Board of Inland Revenue.

Most of these and other similar local organizations are concerned with the detailed execution of national policies, but most of them do things which have local consequences, but for which they are not directly responsible to any local body. On the other hand, they are sometimes amenable to local influences: the fact that some health and welfare services are provided by local councils makes it certain that Regional Hospital Boards will be in constant communication with local authorities, and similarly the existence of a right of appeal to a local panel against a valuation forces the valuers to take some account of local conditions.

Sub-managements of Nationalized Industries

The organizations for making transport, gas and electricity locally available are an important segment of local administration. Like the provincial offices of ministries the sub-managements are not locally responsible, but at least there are local consultative committees alongside them. Unfortunately the detailed layouts of these industries are the haphazard result of history: they bear no relationship to each other and are sometimes not even internally integrated. This is especially true of the transport networks in which bus services are not necessarily co-ordinated with railways, with each other or with privately owned concerns.

Specialist Bodies and Police

A number of local services are managed by specialist bodies of different sorts. Land drainage, for instance, is under a more-or-less uniform system of drainage boards and water conservation authorities, but water supply is variously (depending on locality) in the hands of local authorities, or of water boards or even of commercial undertakings subjected to limitations on their profits. Markets and harbour services are equally unstandardized: the former are mostly still provided under ancient charters; the latter by boards of commissioners appointed under local legislation. The most famous harbour authorities are probably the Port of London Authority and the Tyne Improvement Commissioners; the jurisdiction of the Yarmouth Port and Haven Commissioners covers the whole of the Norfolk Broads.

By far the most important specialist authority, however, is the police authority. It is a curious and interesting fact that there is no national police or gendarmerie and that the Home Secretary's powers extend to appointments, pay and equipment but do not include a power of command. A constable holds a public office for whose exercise he is *personally* responsible; he must use his own judgement and must not obey an illegal order for he can be brought to book for abuse of his functions. Though he holds these independent powers he is subject to police discipline and paid by a police authority. In most parts this is a joint committee of one or several county or county borough councils together with magistrates for the same area, but in Greater London (except the City) it is the Commissioner of Metropolitan Police, appointed by the Home Secretary, and in the City it is the Court of Aldermen, all of whom are magistrates *ex-officio*.

The 'Local Government' System

Outside Greater London, which has arrangements peculiar to itself, England and Wales has six basic types of authority and some variants. The six are the county, the county borough, the non-county borough, the urban district, the rural district and the rural parish. Apart from a large minority of the smallest rural parishes each of these has an elected council exercising powers conferred upon it by Act of Parliament and (with minor exceptions) none of these bodies can exercise any power not so conferred. The system is most commonly misunderstood because of this – the so-called *ultra vires* – rule: powers must be paid for and the Magna Carta principle that no one shall have his property taken away except in accordance with law means in local government that a council must produce a specific statutory authority for every expenditure of public funds. This restraining principle is responsible for much apparent lack of initiative: there are many admirable things which local authorities would like to do but for which they have no statutory power.

The second fundamental basis of local government is that (again with minor exceptions) the principle of specialization applies. The small authorities are not supervised by or subordinate to the larger nor are they subordinate to the government. The difference between them is that each class of authority has functions suitable to itself and exercises them independently of the others. In fact some functions are carried out by authorities in more than one class, but this does not invalidate the principle.

Beginning with an open country divided into rural parishes some parts are so sparsely populated that they need no council at all and require only that there should be some simple and official means of calling the inhabitants together to express their wishes. Other parishes, however, have villages in varying stages of development and these will have sufficient people and resources to support a parish council capable of providing such things as a public hall and playing fields and able to look after various public properties like a village green.

For larger services requiring staffs and capital such as housing, sewerage and refuse collection a larger unit is required; this is the rural district. Scattered about in this landscape, however, there will be substantial market towns; if these were merely parishes their representation on the rural district councils would be so large that they would be able to attract most of the district expenditure to the town; therefore

101

these towns are separately administered as urban districts or non-county boroughs (the difference is chiefly ceremonial) and within the town their councils have the functions of parish and rural district councils added together.

There are, however, some services such as roads and education which are so costly that only a very large unit can afford them, or are of a nature that they can only function on a wide basis: planning is an example of this. Accordingly, an aggregation of urban and rural districts will form a county whose council administers these widespread or very expensive services. Next, in various parts of the country there are great cities which again are separately administered from their surrounding counties and their councils exercise all the powers of parish, district and county councils. Lastly there are certain great urban concentrations such as the Black Country where several towns have grown into each other; these, like London, have special arrangements suited to their size and peculiarities.

This simplified description needs to be qualified. Firstly many of the units are ancient, but populations have lately grown or moved. Hence places formerly important have declined and others have grown. Some parishes have more than one village; others should have been urban districts long ago. There are boroughs and urban districts which are mere villages while others have been of county borough size for sometime and so forth.

The history of recent efforts to reorganize local government provides an example of the importance of inertia in public affairs. Some changes were made in 1933, but progress ended with the Second World War. Negotiations between the English local authority associations on future reform began in 1944 and continued acrimoniously until 1956. The government imposed a compromise and set up Local Government Commissions to deal with counties and county boroughs in England and Wales in 1959. By 1966 the Welsh Commission had failed to produce proposals acceptable in the principality; the English Commission produced some solutions in important areas such

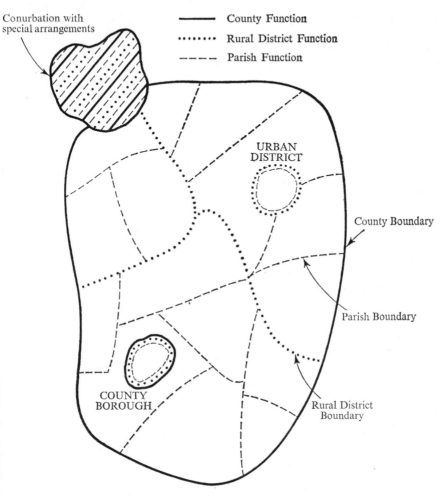

Fig. 9. LOCAL AUTHORITIES

as Tyneside, but the whole process had been overtaken by the population explosion, and a new Royal Commission was proposed with greatly extended powers. It seems unlikely that the geographical regroupings will be complete before 1976.

The second complication is that some urban authorities are ancient chartered corporations whose traditions and resources differ from those of urban districts. Hence boroughs have slightly more power than urban districts and similarly county boroughs than county councils.

Thirdly there are many local Acts of Parliament conferring special powers on particular councils. Most of these apply to counties and county boroughs and only a minority to other kinds of council.

Fourthly, as will appear, the financial resources of local authorities are not sufficient to support their work, so they receive large grants from the government.

Lastly, as already mentioned, the powers of the various classes of authority to some extent overlap. The details of the allotment of powers appear in the table opposite.

Constitution of Councils

The local government electorate is similar to the parliamentary electorate except that certain property owners in a council area can vote in that council's election. Save in most parishes councillors are elected by wards; they all hold office for three years. In boroughs every ward has three seats of which one is refilled each year; in some districts there is a similar annual turnover but by rotation of wards or parishes. Boroughs and county councils have, in addition, aldermen equal in number to one third of the councillors and elected by the latter for six years at a time, half being elected every three years. Every Council appoints a chairman annually; in a borough he is, however, called the Mayor or Lord Mayor.

In the City of London the constitution is radically different. The 'common council-men' are elected for one year only; the

	County Borough	County	Non-County Borough	Urban District	Rural District	Parish
Aerodromes	F	F	F	F	F	
Allotments	F		F	F		F
Cemeteries and Crematoria	F		F	F	F	F
Children	F	F				
Civic Restaurants	F		F	F	F	
Coast Protection	C	I	C	C	C	
Civil Defence	F	F	M	M	M	
Diseases of Animals	F	F	S			
Education	F	F	DS	DS		M
Entertainment	F		F	F	F	
Fire Brigade	F	F				
Food and Drugs	F	F	F	F		
Swimming Pools	F		F	F	F	F
Halls and Community Centres	F		F	F	F	F
Health	F	F	D	D	D	M
Highways	F	F	M	M		M
Housing	F		F	F	F	
Libraries	F	F	M	M		
Lighting	F	M	F	F	FS	FS
Markets	F		M	M	M	
Registration of Vehicles	F	F				
Parks, etc.	F	F	F	F	F	F
Refuse Collection	F		F	F	F	M
Sewerage	F		F	F	F	
Supervision of Shops	F	F	F	F		
Small Holdings		F				
Town and Country Planning	F	F	D	D	D	
Weights and Measures	F	F	S		S	
Welfare	F	F	D	D	D	

Fig. 10. POWERS OF LOCAL AUTHORITIES
F = Full. D = Delegated. M = Minor. I = Indirect.
C = Coastal only. S = Sometimes

aldermen are elected by the electorate at large and for life, but the aldermen as a body have a veto on the election of a new alderman. The proportion of aldermen is much smaller. The Lord Mayor must be an alderman but is chosen by the representatives of the guilds from two candidates offered by the Court of Aldermen. Finally, there are certain purposes for which the aldermen must sit apart and decide matters separately from the Common Council as a whole.

Every council appoints a clerk (who is its first servant) and other chief officers depending on its powers and needs. It also appoints committees to which its various functions are allotted for management through the appropriate chief officer. Often a council delegates almost its entire responsibility on a given subject so that a full council considers that committee's business only formally and in connection with the annual budget. This makes it difficult for the public to discover what is happening, for committee meetings are not usually open to the public while council meetings, though public, are sometimes dull and difficult to follow.

Local Authority Finance

Council expenditure generally is covered from four major sources, namely, rates, loans, payments and grants. The proportion of each of these to the total naturally varies from year to year and with the situation status and policy of the council. In total and over a period of years the four sources of local government finance have been roughly equal, but the differences in detail are, as will be seen, considerable.

The basic resource is the rate, which is a tax levied on the annual value of property other than agricultural land. Obviously concentrations of new houses and factories will produce great variations in the wealth and therefore in the standard of service provided by councils. Accordingly, the government makes grants to those counties and county boroughs whose average rateable value is below the national average; in addition they receive specific grants for particular purposes which generally reflect the policy of the government of the day. The grant system is thus at the mercy of the tides of national politics; it has in fact suffered three major changes since 1947. Thirdly there is a separate system of grants for road building. Part (25 per cent) of the first two grants (but not the road grants) is passed on to district and non-county borough councils. Income from these grants usually exceeds income from rates.

There is also a new form of grant whose purpose is to relieve poorer ratepayers of some of the burden of paying rates, but as it only covers half the relief which such a ratepayer can claim, the other half has to be borne by the other ratepayers in the area.

Local authorities borrow for capital purposes only and so their indebtedness will depend upon whether they have undertaken substantial capital works or not. Boroughs and districts have, for instance, for many years been building houses on borrowed funds. The sums raised in this way are very large and in addition to the usual methods of raising loans through the money market, all local authorities can borrow from the government through the Public Works Loans Board, and parish councils can borrow from county councils.

Lastly local authorities receive large sums for services rendered by them. Much the largest item under this heading is rent for houses.

Regional Bodies and Functional Subdivisions

A region is bigger than a county but smaller than the kingdom. Northern Ireland, Scotland and Wales are genuine regions with institutions peculiar to themselves as such. As has already been indicated many public services are organized upon a geographical basis which takes no account of local government boundaries or indeed each other's. For instance the so-called railway and hospital regions, the ecclesiastical provinces, the Divisional organization of the Ministry of Transport, the military commands, and the increasing number of combined police authorities have nothing in common. These are not, properly speaking, regions at all but functional subdivisions.

In 1965 however a new type of regional organization came into existence. This was concerned with economic planning and consisted of eight regions each with an Advisory Council and a Regional Economic Planning Board. Both bodies are appointed by the government, the members of the Board being mostly civil servants from ministries with local interests. and those of the Advisory Council being persons with local knowledge, In theory they have no executive powers and their staffs are minimal; in practice they impose work upon planning authorities, who feel obliged to comply with their requests for information. Moreover they have attracted considerable, if not necessarily justifiable, public prestige and in so far as they have any direct power it consists in being able to influence the government departments.

Since economic planning is a dominating activity capable of affecting most of the work of any local authority subject to it, it seems as if a new type of sub-government – not locally responsible – is in the making.

14

VOLUNTEERS AND VOLUNTARY ORGANIZATIONS INVOLVED IN ADMINISTRATION

Many local services could not be carried on without the help of the tens of thousands of charities and other societies which exist in all parts of the country. These have been mentioned already, but whereas in national affairs they mostly protect an outlook or interest, at the local level they form a working and usually unpaid part of the machine. The principle of voluntary participation in public life runs very deep: neither councillors, for instance, nor Justices of the Peace nor school managers are paid. So also there is an endless variety of organizations concerned with some aspect of public benefit manned by volunteers and financed mostly by gifts though sometimes by grants from public funds; these vary from sports clubs and village hall committees to such well-known bodies as Councils of Social Service, and the Family Welfare Association and they cater for most of the difficult aspects of life. Thus infirm old people will be helped at least as often by voluntary organizations as by the welfare authorities, and indeed the statutory and voluntary bodies will exchange information and patients. Similar situations exist in child welfare, in education and in such social matters as music and drama.

In all parts of local life these organizations perform in varying degrees three valuable public functions. They stimulate both the public and the authorities; they supplement the official services; and they collect and provide information. As public services have expanded since the Second World

War the need for voluntary societies has increased rather than otherwise. The reason for this not wholly expected fact is that there are many things which it is difficult for an official, with his public status and regulated habits, to do properly and therefore the more official activity the more there is for the volunteer. This is especially true of 'social' services, such as child care, which require a high degree of human understanding; officials must be guided by rules because otherwise they would cease to be servants and become masters, but situations constantly appear where official rules cannot apply. Here it is the volunteer who can do most good.

The idea of the 'trust', that is, the concept of property or money managed voluntarily by someone for a purpose which does not benefit him but someone else is a characteristic and indeed a remarkable feature of English public and private life. It is, for instance, a matter of astonishment to foreigners that the life-boats are run in this way with perfect efficiency and without official control or government funds. And few other countries have institutions remotely resembling the Nuffield Foundation, or the Carnegie United Kingdom Trust. But this sort of work is also done on a vast scale at much humbler levels; no census of trusts has ever been undertaken but in 1967 the number of voluntary associations with funds *in rural areas alone* exceeded 50,000. It is probable that the number of people acting as trustees runs into seven figures.

The management of public affairs in Britain is almost unintelligible if no attention is paid to this voluntary element and our institutions at all levels would have to be quite different – and more expensive – without it.

15

CONSTITUTIONAL AMENDMENT

Where a country has a written constitution it can be amended only by some procedure not normally applicable to ordinary legislation. This is not the case in the United Kingdom (save locally in Northern Ireland) but the distinction between the written and unwritten or between the specially protected and the flexible is not, probably, as important as has sometimes been thought. The reason is that the constitutional law of a country is only one part or major element of its constitution. There are always others. The ruling group is found everywhere; the central organs of sovereignty are found in most countries, though their pattern may differ; and the same is true of instruments of government. There may be other fundamental elements such as the special position formerly accorded to the armed forces in Japan, or the influence of an international obligation such as the Treaty of Rome in the Common Market Countries, or the Customs union between Switzerland and Liechtenstein. Such treaties are increasingly influencing constitutional development even in the United Kingdom by subtracting important subjects (such as tariffs) from national initiative and sovereignty. In addition, here at least, there is one element which is enormously important, and seldom discussed, namely the Time Factor.

It follows that any change made in any of the four, five or more major elements of a constitution is a constitutional amendment. *It is impossible to exaggerate the importance of this, for it is largely unknown to the public;* it is mainly changes requiring some spectacular operation such as the passage of a controversial bill which excite public attention. The rest is apt to go by default. Moreover constitutional amendment is taking place gradually all the time by the operation of natural events or the side effects of policies or legislation. The death of a figure such as Sir Winston Churchill is a constitutional event because it perceptibly altered (amongst other things) the atmosphere of The 5000. The creation of a new social service diverts volunteers to other public interests, and changes the balance of their attitude to public affairs.

This 'accidental' but constant movement should serve as a warning of the remarkable ease with which the constitution can be altered, not only without recourse to public formalities but in such a way that when it is necessary to resort to them the result is a foregone conclusion.

Changes within The 5000

Any measure which substantially alters the composition of The 5000 is a constitutional amendment. Such changes can be sudden or slow, the former being easier to detect than the latter, and they can be made by formal or informal methods. For example the creation almost a century ago of a paid statutory civil service recruited by examination has slowly introduced into The 5000 a body of individuals who are strong because of their corporate background, numerous as compared with many other of the components, and formidable for their abilities. This has changed the manner of our public affairs almost out of recognition – from the drafting of bills, and the organization of the instruments of government to the shaping of the public revenues. Yet these consequences have flowed from an ordinary act of parliament concerned primarily with efficiency and avoidance of administrative corruption.

But it is possible to interfere in the composition of The 5000 a great deal more easily and quickly than this. A conspicuous recent example is the rise into prominence of the academic expert. Formerly, and for the most part, professors wrote books and their influence, never negligible, was channelled through the public media of the written or spoken word. This, of course, continues, but now many individual academics have entered The 5000 simply because the decision makers have acquired a habit of consulting them. This amendment has been made without any formality and (save in the case of one or two individuals) without public knowledge or protest, yet it is significant because it brings into our working institutions an element which is valuable because intellectual, but divorced from responsibility.

Changes in the Machine of Sovereignty

British constitutional history has often been recounted in terms of changes in the balance of authority between the Crown, the Houses of Parliament and the judiciary, but the rise of the modern political party with its strict discipline has altered yet again the functioning of the central organs without a single change in the law. The modern Prime Minister is a more powerful personage, so long as he can rely on popular support, than any monarch since Queen Elizabeth I. The Sovereign takes his advice; the complexion of the House of Lords can be changed overnight or its powers of delay over-ridden; and the House of Commons is managed through a majority which is seldom anything but docile. This ministerial dictatorship still has its limitations and safeguards against abuse but these are wearing thin. In March 1966 the Commons protested against the established practice of retroactive legislation, and then only because a Minister meant to use powers which he had not got, but which six months before the government said that it intended to ask Parliament to create. An usurpation was avoided. The 'Ombudsman' and his staff were paid during 1966 without any legal sanction whatever. This time an usurpation was not avoided, and when the Commons provided in December 1966 that the new morning sessions could not be counted out they enabled the government to do some business in the presence of no one but the speaker. Is this parliamentary government at all?

In fact changes in the central organs are made often, and frequently without serious difficulty even when the most formal public processes have to be employed. Ministries are created or reallocated by Orders in Council of which the public hears nothing. An Act of 1935 required a small proportion of paid ministers to be peers; this was evaded in 1963 by appointing unpaid ministers in the Commons. In both World Wars the Cabinet was reduced to a small body simply by the Prime Minister tendering the requisite advice to the Crown. Since 1910 the powers and composition of both Houses have been altered several times; constituency boundaries are under constant review; the electorate has been twice increased by the inclusion of women successively over thirty and then over twenty-one, and twice decreased by disfranchising soldiers under twenty-one and by a change in the compilation of electoral registers which disfranchises many voters under twenty-two.

Changes in the Time Factor

If it is so easy to alter other parts of the constitution a rule which forces governments to put their policies in an order of priority and compels them to consult outside interests as far as possible becomes a paramount safeguard against oppression. Such a rule is to be found in the requirement that as Parliament is a corporation called (usually annually) into being by summons and 'killed' by prorogation every proposal must have passed through every stage of parliamentary gestation before the 'death' if it is to endure as law. The habitual prolongation of sessions, as in 1966, would be a profound and possibly subversive alteration.

The time available in a parliamentary session is not large. Therefore the rules which govern its use and allocation are constitutionally vital. The many stages through which a bill must pass are laid down by the common law of Parliament; they ought probably to be altered only by legislation but though they are based upon centuries of experience and convenience major changes in them are not as unlikely to occur as was previously assumed. The manner in which the bills go through a stage and the time allocated to each is treated as procedural, governed by rules made by each House and capable of alteration by a simple resolution of the House concerned. It is possible for procedural changes to be so far reaching that they invade and transform the realm of the substantive or legal. Constitutional amendments of this sort can be made easily and are made often. A number of instances will illustrate their importance.

At the end of the last century (as a result of Irish obstruction) the Commons began to pass resolutions setting out a timetable for the stages of a bill regardless of anything which a member might wish to say or of any amendments which had been put down. The corollary of this was that it became necessary to impose upon the Speaker the burden of selecting those amendments for which time could be found. This function he, of course, exercises judicially having regard to merits and whether the issue raised has been recently discussed. The result is that many questions which members desire to raise (often at the request of outside interests) never get a hearing at all and outside interests tend to approach government departments direct in the hope of securing their point in the original bill or by means of a government sponsored amendment. This has diminished the status of the private member and increased that of the civil servant. It may also have helped to increase the numbers of White Papers: the discussion on these documents helps to avoid mistakes in the subsequent bill.

Since the Second World War the Commons have habitually (but not invariably) sent bills 'upstairs' to be considered by standing committees instead of taking the committee stage 'on the floor' of the whole House. This has greatly enlarged the time available for legislation, because committee stages on half a dozen bills can proceed simultaneously, and because committees meet in the morning whereas the *full* House begins its

I

sittings in the afternoon. But this in its turn has helped to change the complexion of the House and seems to be leading to the rise of a class of professional politicians. Till recently members could be and were paid on a part-time basis because, with a little luck, their parliamentary duties might not impose upon their time before three or four o'clock in the afternoon – even if they then had to sit all night. The private member could earn an independent living which made him less amenable to party discipline and brought into the House a width of current experience from ordinary life. There has, of course, always been the member without private means, but he has usually received support from a pressure group and was, to that extent, a professional politician. The modern problem is the member without *time*, and this was solved (if that is the right word) in 1963 by paying a full-time salary: in other words modern members think that they must devote themselves to politics, and judging by newspaper comment, most of the public thinks so too. Nothing of the sort has happened in British history before, and though it is too early to predict the consequences, foreign experience suggests that party politics may become more bitter as the competition for salaried posts becomes fiercer. It would probably have been better to give them a free secretary each at the public expense.

Under the first Attlee administration (1945–50) the Commons decided that government business should take precedence on all sitting days. This prevented private members from introducing bills and put all legislation in the hands of the government. This resolution, combined with a policy of taking committee stages upstairs and a determined use of timetables and closures gave the government enough parliamentary time within which to pass the series of controversial bills to nationalize coal, steel, transport, electricity and gas. Without the aid of these easily made constitutional amendments they could not possibly all have been done before the next general election foreshadowed the fall of the government.

In 1966 the government proposed to transform the character of the Prices and Incomes Bill by including in it penal measures of a kind never contemplated since the Middle Ages. In order to rush the new provisions through they were introduced as amendments in a standing committee so that in effect they never received a second reading in the Commons. A motion to bring the bill on to the floor of the house was defeated and in the meantime the Lords were invited to debate a document containing a version of the bill still in the Commons but altered as if the Commons had amended it in the way the government wished. It is not yet clear how serious will be the consequences of this attempt both to blur the second reading and Committee procedures and to alter the functions of a second House, but evidently it represents an important inroad on the time factor and in addition a severe curtailment of the right to debate principles.

Efficiency was the pretext or justification of all these amendments and indeed the so-called inefficiency of Parliament is a frequent subject of public comment. If speed and efficiency are equated the argument is misconceived; the quickest way to promulgate and enforce a policy is to rule as a dictator by decree – subject perhaps to a parliamentary rubber stamp. This is the ultimate result of too much tampering with the time factor: in two cases of nationalization – steel and transport – the result was not efficiency, and both industries have been subjected to legislative tinkering ever since.

Overseas Engagements

Overseas engagements raise three different sorts of issue. The 'private relationship' with the Commonwealth makes it difficult to alter the international position of the Crown without the consent (or more exactly the advice) of the independent Commonwealth Governments. Secondly, though the conduct of foreign policy is in the hands of the Crown it cannot make any treaty which might alter the law without the passage of the required Act. Thirdly, an agreement once made, especially one involving legislation, restricts the power of the Government or Parliament (as the case may be) to alter its policy or the law unilaterally in a manner inconsistent with the agreement.

Notwithstanding the legal supremacy of the Crown in Parliament there are in fact certain legislative operations which it cannot undertake without the consent of foreign powers. For instance, though Commonwealth Preference continues to exist the United Kingdom is prevented by treaty from manipulating its tariff system so as to increase that preference as compared with other nations. Legislation to break this rule would be enforceable inside the kingdom, but would provoke sanctions by foreign countries which would so damage the economy that it would never be introduced. The parallel between this type of sanction in international affairs and the financial sanction used by the Commons to control the policy of the Monarch is obvious.

Changes in the Instruments of Government

It is primarily through the instruments of government that the citizen experiences government at all, and he is sensitive to changes made in them. If something such as a death has to be registered it matters whether the registry is far or near and open at the right times, and whether the process is easy and sympathetic or troublesome and bureaucratic. The same is true of legal proceedings, of the collection of taxes, and of the behaviour of nationalized industries and local authorities. Generally speaking changes tending towards greater efficiency and more sympathy will bring more public support for the system as a whole, and those apparently in the opposite direction will do the reverse. Thus the extent to which the constitution is tolerated by the masses of the people is related to the form of the instruments, and the burden of activity and cost which they impose.

This being so one might expect that it would not be too difficult to adjust the instruments to changing circumstances, and theoretically (or in law) this is the case, but in practice they show a remarkable capacity for resistance to change. From the Middle Ages the law was administered by several independent Courts of Record which were not supposed to know each other's business and which were amalgamated only as recently as 1875. Local government has been in the throes of geographical reorganization since 1946 and the process is not at an end. No one has yet found a successful method of co-ordinating public transport; and it has taken half a century to reform company taxation.

There are two paramount reasons for this: inertia and vested interest. It is unfortunate that both these terms have acquired uncomplimentary meanings for both have their beneficent, or at least disinterested aspect.

Government, after all, provides a framework for ordinary life and most people are busy earning their competence and living their private lives. It exists to serve the citizens, not the other way round. Established habits are useful because they save mental and physical effort. Thus ordinary people will oppose closely spaced changes in the instruments of government because they will have repeatedly to devote time and energy to rearranging their habits. The introduction of capital gains taxes requires permanent records of the prices at which shares are bought and sold. This was previously unnecessary; millions of such transactions take place every year; someone has to do the work. A change in the organization of housing authorities may result in thousands of tenants having to pay their rent by a different method or to a different person. The constant changes in the details of administration are already bewildering enough and have been the main reason for the establishment of the Citizens Advice Bureaux.

The second important feature of administration which tends to retard change is that it involves a vast number of detailed

119

and often repetitive actions which cannot be carried out without large staffs. Governments (whether central or local) are easily the biggest employers. In 1966 central departments alone employed 804,000 people. Thus radical changes would affect the lives and families of great numbers within the system as well as disturbing the habits of the rest. Most of these people have votes.

Safety Devices

The ease with which most parts of our constitution can be amended naturally raises the question whether it is safe against the ambitions of any particular group on the one hand or against disruptive and anarchical forces on the other. For a variety of reasons, some bad but many good, the government of the Kingdom has for many years shown a centralizing and standardizing tendency: services administered on a small scale have been transferred to larger units which in their turn have lost functions to the central government, and nearly all the most important work of local administration is now in the hands of local representatives of national bodies. This movement seems to be continuing and one of its effects will probably be to enlarge The 5000 and increase its importance; but it is precisely in this that a danger may lurk. The curb on overweening ambition lies in the diversity of membership of The 5000 and in their differences of interest, outlook and policy. A development which tends to greater homogeneity or which introduces an excessively numerous and well equipped element is or may become a danger to liberty because once The 5000 are in total agreement or are purged of dissident elements, nothing except armed revolt or a general strike can stop them from employing the resources of the nation for any purpose they please. This closing of the ranks has happened twice in fifty years to fight the world wars: government was conducted dictatorially and the nation accepted the position because a military crisis requires a military system. Such a dictatorship in peacetime might establish itself if the nation were somehow induced to believe that it was threatened by a grave (possibly economic) danger but actually such a case is more likely to arise through a purge: a situation, that is, where an element in The 5000 succeeds in expelling or bribing all its opponents. Since the kingdom is no longer likely to undertake an aggressive foreign war it is probable or even inevitable that the nation's resources would then be used against a part or class of the nation itself. This is revolution, even if not accompanied by the excesses associated with such catastrophes; indeed the French Revolution was of this character.

The second question is whether The 5000 are secure against attack from outside: that is to say whether there is much chance that anyone can expel or destroy all of them and replace them with entirely new men. Clearly it would need a large well-knit, devoted, revolutionary and single-minded organization to do this, and such a body would have to be able to secure widespread and well placed support. Once the new men were in power the nation's resources would be employed, again, against parts of the nation itself. The Russian Revolution (at least before the rise of Stalin) seems to have been of this type. In the last and worst analysis power stays in the hands of those who control the machine-guns, but before a machine-gun situation arises much can happen. Discontent can take many forms not apparently related to politics; military disaster apart, it is not the discontent of the weak and starving that overthrows governments but the determination of the well-off and well-fed. The English Peasants' Revolt and the French Jacquerie failed; the prosperous revolutionaries of France in 1789 and Japan in 1869 succeeded.

From this point of view it might be argued that material exists for an explosion. It is difficult to deny that the kingdom is prosperous as never before and that that prosperity is widely distributed. The young – the next generation of citizens – have money in an abundance never before experienced, but a rising crime rate and a marked dissociation from political and moral attitudes of earlier generations indicate a malaise of which discontent at the holding of the 1966 elections was a symptom. On the other hand there seems to be no organization able to focus these discontents into a violent threat to society as a whole. It seems to follow that action is needed to forestall the rise of such a body, by assuaging the discontents on which it can work; this is unlikely to happen until the new attitudes make themselves felt in The 5000 by the introduction of new and younger blood.

Part Four

EXTERNAL AFFAIRS

16

CIRCUMSTANCES

It is necessary to start with a warning. Every group, whether a football club or nation has relationships as a group with other groups. Nevertheless in public business the distinction between internal and external affairs is somewhat artificial, for the one reacts on the other, and external affairs are conducted with an eye to internal well-being. This is equally true of the distinctions between the different aspects of external affairs, which are as artificial as those used in the analysis of internal institutions; yet they must be made if the subject is to be treated at all. The Circumstances, Objects, Instruments and Trends described in this Part interlace in a single pattern, which is confused if not effaced, if it is disentangled.

On Being an Island

Britain, as an island which does not wholly feed itself, must import its living mostly by sea or send about 40 per cent of its population to live elsewhere, or cease, artificially, to be an island.

So long as it imports its living it must export to pay for it. Therefore the kingdom will need industry, and will have a special interest in cheap foreign raw materials, in overseas markets, in the maintenance of an efficient and large overseas transport service, and in easy access by that service to the ports and airfields of the world.

The search for self-sufficiency through migration is probably a wild-goose chase because it would reduce the productivity of industry more quickly than it reduced home demand, and it would alter the balance of ages in the population since receiving countries do not like to accept elderly migrants. In fact for over twenty years there has been a shortage of labour and an inflow of migrants; nevertheless there has been during the same period a noticeable outflow (mostly to Canada and Australia) of the energetic and enterprising. The population of Australia was increased by net migration between 1960 and 1964 by nearly 390,000. Many of these came from the United Kingdom.

It is now easier than formerly for Britain to cease to be an island and the temptations to try it will not have been lessened by the seamen's strike of 1966. The British and French electricity grids are already connected and exchange power daily. The Channel Tunnel is technically feasible and one day the kingdom will doubtless enter the Common Market. This might divert transatlantic trade from continental to British ports for direct forwarding to European recipients; it would give the continental farmer a new market here and British industry a vast new market on the continent.

The Neighbourhood of Europe

It was British policy to maintain an European balance which would save this vast land mass within sight of Dover from domination by a hostile power. This is still an objective but the definition of power has changed. The wars and revolutions of the last half century have demolished every European power except Russia, by whom Europe is likely to be dominated if it does not unite. Union will convert Europe into a power in its own right and many steps towards unity have already been taken. If Britain remains outside, the union may one day become hostile. The logic of the policy of balance may be summarized as 'If you can't beat 'em, join 'em.'

The geographical situation contains many detailed features of high importance, but of these it is proposed to select only two. The nearest European country is France, with whom British relationships have been uneasy for centuries. French temperament and French ambitions have shown a tendency to collide (despite all mutual compliments) with British since the early middle ages and it is idle to pretend that the two nations get on easily or understand each other now. The French have taken a leading part in and have given their particular colouring to the movement towards European unity: it will require the utmost patience and forbearance amongst all the parties to create a workable federation which includes the United Kingdom.

Secondly, at Yalta in 1945 the Russians persuaded their allies into a geographical settlement of central Europe which was calculated to perpetuate the tensions between East and West and so to force the East European States to rely upon Russian protection and be subject to her domination.

The 'older Germany' was partitioned in a way which was intended to give lasting offence to German sentiment: Königsberg, the coronation place of the Prussian Kings, is now, as Kaliningrad, a Russian town. Other places with strong emotional positions in the German mind such as Danzig (Gdansk), Stettin (Szeczin), and the Neumark were handed over to Poland, and Berlin lies surrounded by a zone where a Communist régime is kept in power solely by Russian machine-guns and whence there is a constant flow of refugees across the mined barbed wire of the Iron Curtain.

However peaceable the West German Federal Government may be in its intentions, the recovery of these or most of these lost territories is a fundamental objective which its public opinion would never allow it to abandon; the refugees are numerous (they run into millions) and vocal, and in any event they could not be forgotten because every German taxpayer has to pay a special tax to support and rehabilitate them.

This is one of the reasons why the union of Europe must proceed slowly. The other countries would be unlikely to back Germany in a military attempt on Poland, but if they forcibly restrained her the political stability of Western Germany would end. Only time can heal these wounds.

The Old and New Commonwealth

A special factor in the external situation is the Commonwealth, which consists of two parts: the states settled by populations of European, predominantly British, origin ('The Old Commonwealth') and the former conquered but now independent States ('The New Commonwealth') inhabited mostly by indigenous peoples. The Sovereign reigns in the former and in only a decreasing number of the latter, but the remainder still accord an indefinable primacy to the British Crown: it was said of the enthusiastic welcome which Queen Elizabeth II received in republican India that 'She is the only Queen they've got.'

The relationship, then, is partly emotional but it is also economic, customary and strategic. In the imperial days important links of commerce and finance were built up and later protected through the British customs legislation known then as imperial and later as commonwealth preference. These links have not been wholly superseded, though the preferences cannot now be strengthened. British order and trade brought the English language and most of the principles of English law. These, again, survive to a considerable extent. They form a common background with that of the United Kingdom, but, it must be added, they facilitate the economic penetration of the Commonwealth by that other country with the same background, the United States of America.

Strategically the Commonwealth is still important. There are still United Kingdom bases in many distant parts of the world from Gibraltar to Hong Kong, but the independent States themselves maintain forces and bases which are not negligible. It is perhaps here that the distinction between the old and new Commonwealth is most significant. An armed clash between the countries of the old Commonwealth is highly unlikely: but, as the Rhodesian affair has shown, the new Commonwealth has fewer temperamental grounds for loyalty to an older idea.

The Rise of the Native

Until the turn of the century imperialism was a respectable, indeed a praiseworthy, notion. It was communism which turned it into a jargon word of abuse, and associated with it the idea of military power used to secure foreign markets and labour. History only sometimes but not often supports the Communist contention, and in any event the British colonial period was not all loss to a colony. By 1945 the only empires left were those of France, Britain, Portugal, Belgium and Russia. In the creation of the United Nations Organization an undertaking had to be given by participants that colonial régimes would, under United Nations supervision, prepare their territories for independence which would eventually be granted. Russia was militarily strong enough to prevent the colonial status of her vast non-Russian territories from being established, and both Russia and the United States had an interest in the liquidation of other colonialisms – each wanted to penetrate these areas, the Americans for an economic, the Russians for a revolutionary purpose.

The movement towards local independence had also received enormous impetus from the destruction by the Japanese of the American, British, Dutch and French régimes in South East Asia and its great islands. There was little chance of these governments being re-established and the four powers, who spoke a great deal of liberation in their wartime propaganda, made a virtue of necessity and retreated, though at different times and speeds. It was consistent with this that Africa should follow the same course; the signature of the United Nations Charter was on this ground alone a world-shaking event, for three of its founders, the United Kingdom, Belgium and France, were formally committed to the orderly abandonment of political control over most of a continent. It is difficult to convey the vast scale of this undertaking: but it is farther from Tangier (within sight of Spain) to Cape Town than it is from London to Darjeeling: and there are thirty-three new African

129

countries with 250 million souls. This process has advanced with occasional bloodshed but, save in the Congo and Algeria, on a riot rather than a civil war scale. This was the best that could be reasonably expected and the peaceful nature of the transfer was due mainly to British and eventually French recognition of the dangers of delay. It has, however, covered the continent with governments and political systems which are weak to the point of instability.

Humanly speaking the British handover in Southern Asia was on an even vaster scale. The five new states of India, Pakistan, Ceylon, Burma and Malaysia contained 530 million people. The strength and stability of their régimes seem to be standing up to stiffer tests than those of Africa.

The Marxist Great Powers

It is not necessary in connection with international affairs to discuss the social merits of communism, but only its methods. All Communists agree upon two not wholly reconcilable propositions: namely the deterministic doctrine that violent revolution is inevitable in a capitalist country, and the free will doctrine that Communists everywhere must work ceaselessly to bring it about. They disagree inevitably about methods: the primary issue being whether or not a Communist State should use its armed power to impose revolution abroad. From their own point of view there is much to be said (and said and said) on both sides; on the one hand it may be deemed praiseworthy to bring the blessings of communism to the toiling millions as soon as possible: on the other, war is destructive and encourages the very nationalism which is believed to be a capitalist vice.

But Communist statesmen are as much liable to the temptations of power as any others, and on the whole the two Communist great powers have pursued a course of international aggression when it seemed that they might benefit. Russia began in 1920 with the unsuccessful attack on Poland, the

130

repression of Ukrainian, and Caucasian separatism, and the reacquisition of an empire in Mohammedan central Asia; and continued during and after the Second World War with the conquest and subversion of nine east European countries. China unsuccessfully attacked South Korea, and conquered Tibet; and in imposing its will upon Inner Mongolia and Sinkiang came into conflict with Russia which was trying to penetrate both these areas itself. There were, moreover, other grounds of dispute, for the Russians had learnt about atomic bombs and rocketry and knew of their effects, whereas the Chinese regarded Western military power as a 'paper tiger'. The Russians therefore sought to restrain the Chinese from foreign adventures, such as their military raid on India in 1962.

Marxism provides no solution to problems of mutual opposition between Communist States because it is implicit in it that the situation cannot arise. Logically enough, therefore, the Chinese in the 1960s began to accuse the Russians of not being really Communist. From this dispute no non-Communist Government should seek much comfort: the issue at bottom is not whether the Communist great powers should or should not attack the West, for aggression has already proved so profitable that they are unlikely to abjure it. The question is how they should do so and when.

The Americas

The Americas stretch almost from pole to pole but speak only three major languages. The areas speaking English (U.S.A. and Canada) and Portuguese (Brazil) show a tendency towards unification: the Spanish a high degree of separatism and fragmentation. On the other hand the English areas are politically stable while the Latin countries are not and the two English countries are permanently at peace whereas some of the Latin states periodically fight each other. The differences between the Latin and the English States are heightened in a variety of

K   131

other ways. The culture of the former is partly Mediterranean and Roman Catholic passed through an Iberian filter: the culture of the latter is north European and Protestant; and if talent and erudition reach the same levels everywhere, the average standard of education is far higher among the English than the Latins.

Overshadowing everything is the tremendous industrial and commercial predominance of the United States not only in America but in the world. The profits of their economy have so far sufficed to provide the armed backbone of resistance to the aggressions of the great Marxist powers, and to sustain a high rate of private investment abroad, and to give financial aid to the so-called developing (or backward) countries. Unless there is a very high rate of return the private investor, even if it is an enormous corporation like General Motors, prefers to risk capital where there are no serious social or political problems; these exist abundantly in Latin America as well as Asia and Africa with the result that the American private investor takes a voluntary interest in stable areas such as Europe and Australia while his government, through foreign aid, attempts compulsorily at his expense to bring stability to backward countries; they do not always appreciate it because of the political influence which it gives to the United States, and save in oilfields (where the ratio of profits to capital is very high) Latin America has less American investment than might at first be expected from its situation and size.

Dominated though the Americas are by the United States, the other countries have always been an unruly brood and are becoming more so, especially in the central area around the Caribbean. The great federal republic of Mexico had a semi-socialist revolution a generation ago and is largely emancipated from the direct internal influence of American big business; the tide has long been setting in the same direction in the smaller States of the central American isthmus so that these tend to receive aid through international agencies (financed mainly with American money) rather than investment. Columbia has been in a state of confusion and local uprising for fifteen years and Cuba has the notorious Communist government of Señor Castro. Moreover the Caribbean is peculiar as being the last area of the Americas to contain colonies: of those still dependent the largest (Puerto Rico) belongs to the United States and the remainder to Britain, Holland and France, the great majority being British.

The Population Explosion

If the world regional problems are vast enough, the world-wide population problem is greater than the sum of them. In the last twenty years medicine has reduced the death-rate so drastically that without any change in the birth-rate at all the world's population in the year 2,000 will be twice that of 1966; this is inevitable and nothing can prevent it. If the distribution of the change were even, the consequences would be damaging enough, but unfortunately the increase in the industrialized West (including Russia) is likely to be only 40 per cent or so, while in underdeveloped Africa, Asia and South America it will probably exceed 100 per cent. Economic growth in the West exceeds population growth: in the underdeveloped territories it lags far behind. Thus the West grows richer while misery piles up elsewhere.

The consequences in terms of the interests of the whole world are unforeseeable in detail but it is obvious that unless some very drastic action is taken there will shortly be a human disaster far surpassing anything hitherto recorded. Nor is this the end of the matter; on present trends the world population is likely to double itself every thirty years after the year 2,000, and most of the newborn will starve. Remedial action apart, if the disaster does not come sooner it will come later.

In these circumstances, and especially with a militant Chinese atomic power quite willing to take serious risks, the great disaster will destroy the levels of civilization in the West and probably its economic ability to rescue the human race.

133

But this economic power is still in being and can be used to turn the scale if it is used resolutely now, and continuously.

Thus there are two essential aims which the West as a whole must drop its differences to pursue. The first (because first in time) is to raise the productivity of the underdeveloped so that it at least keeps pace with their population growth. The second, without which the first will fail in the next century, is to ensure a steady level of world population by the introduction of universal birth control. Programmes of this kind will involve considerable but bearable sacrifices in instalments. The alternative is much worse.

Moreover there is a reasonable probability of success. The world still contains huge untapped resources requiring only capital investment and expertise for exploitation. Ocean fishing, for instance, is still barely past the nomadic hunting stage. Only a small percentage of the world's available water power is as yet harnessed. Vast tracts of land are desert, or under subsistence farming, or unapproachable. The uses of solar radiation are still only the subject of primitive experiment. The danger is that these opportunities will be taken too late.

17

OBJECTS

Trade

The major elements of British overseas trade are seven in number.

Firstly, goods such as furniture or materials such as coal are produced here and sold abroad; secondly, goods such as furs are imported and re-exported at a profit; thirdly, materials such as copper are imported from abroad, converted or incorporated into other things by an industrial process, and exported; fourthly, goods such as food and wine or materials like timber are bought abroad and consumed here; these four are sometimes called the visible operations because they involve solid or visible objects.

Fifthly, there are physical services involving international payments; these include freight paid for the use of ships and aircraft, and payments (for instance to hotels) arising out of the enormous and growing tourist industry. Sixthly, there are the profits which arise because London is an international money market, and the most important of all an international insurance centre. These two, which are very large items, are sometimes called invisible.

A seventh element which is also invisible but is not in the ordinary sense 'trade' is the international movement of funds arising from the need to pay dividends to foreign investors, to pay for installations (such as troops or embassies) which governments maintain abroad, and to make investments in other countries.

The difference over a given period between the cost of and

135

the advantages (in monetary terms) derived from these major elements is known as the balance of payments and generally speaking it is in the interest of the world at large that all countries should maintain (taking one year with another) a roughly even balance. A regular debtor balance in one country forces it in the long run to cut its foreign trade and reduce its standard of living – there is less to buy in the shops. A regular creditor raises its standard and increases its trade but within limits set by its size: a small one can do it for a long time without anyone noticing very much, which accounts for the wealth of a place like Switzerland, but if a big country such as the U.S.A. does it for long it begins to impoverish the rest, and so lays up political trouble or kills the goose that lays the golden eggs. This is one of the explanations for foreign investment and aid. The steady expansion of world prosperity, not to mention American and (to some extent) British trade, could not go on unless some of the profits were ploughed back.

The maintenance of a healthy trade balance obviously involves a great many political and administrative considerations of different kinds. If the balance is adverse the reason may be that the British are bad at selling their products; or that the products are too expensive or delivered too late or of the wrong pattern; or that foreign countries have raised impenetrable tariff or quota barriers; or that too much is being bought at too high a price; or that excessive funds are being exported for investment abroad. Some of the factors can be changed by government action at home such as improving the ports, restricting the export of funds or reducing taxation. Others require action abroad.

Foreign trade policy will, then, involve different considerations represented by different ministries; the most obvious departments concerned are the Foreign and Commonwealth Offices, the Departments of Economic Affairs and Technical Co-operation, the Board of Trade and the armed services. Behind this, however, there is the whole policy-making machine, for foreign and internal policy are closely interwoven. For example, if our motor manufacturers wish to sell cars to a country which wishes to sell wine to us, it may be that no one here will buy the wine unless its price is reduced, so a lowering of the British wine duty may be necessary to enable cars to be sold over there: but the resulting reduction in wine prices might cause a decline in the consumption of beer and so to a lower government revenue from the beer excise. This might have to be offset, for instance, by spending less, by altering the beer excise or by hoping that increased wine drinking will raise the return on the wine duty. Moreover, the introduction of a new competitor into the wine market might make difficulties for countries already exporting wine to us and so perhaps one of these to which the chemical industry has been selling its products now finds that it must buy less of our chemicals. As a result (in our imaginary instance) the Cabinet may have to decide between the competing claims of the motor industry, the chemists and the brewers.

Peace

Trade is impossible without peace. This is true not merely in the international field but within any major country itself. War interrupts communications and diverts industry, labour and ability to destructive ends; civil war destroys the markets where it rages. Peace is not merely a generally or morally desirable thing; it is a special interest of any nation so profoundly dependent upon its trade. Since Tudor times the English talent for waging war (which has always been considerable) has been used less in the service of an aggressive policy as in defence against aggressors. This is the logical attitude of a trading nation, but victory in these conflicts has brought its commercial and territorial prizes and these have not been despised. In this sense it is true that the 'Empire was acquired in a fit of absence of mind'.

Moreover, if peace is the primary condition of prosperity, peace at any price, by definition, cannot be. Questions of honour apart, an aggressor who offered to leave the kingdom alone only if it gave up the profits of its overseas trade would have to be resisted because the population would otherwise starve. This, exactly, represented the war policy of Napoleon and brought about his fall.

On the other hand the kingdom is in no position by itself to enforce a general peace. Powerful it still is, but the U.S.A. and Russia are stronger and a united Europe may become so. The cultivation of appropriate alliances, especially those which tend to keep open the sea lanes, is and always has been a feature of British foreign policy. Wars are commenced by governments who believe that they will win: the object is to create a balance in which no government is likely to believe anything of the sort. Once this is achieved disputes can be settled by other and happier methods.

18

INSTRUMENTS
OF EXTERNAL POLICY

Armed Forces

In an efficiently policed country armed forces exist mainly to support its foreign policy. The guns of Louis XIV were inscribed 'The final argument of Kings'.

The proper management of foreign policy is intricate, but it is also expensive. The last resort of society is the policeman, but the total and prolonged absence of an organized police force eventually leads to disorder: the last resort of international politics is war, but in the absence of international government the disarmed and isolated country tends to fall a victim to armed aggression. Until the advent of effective world government no proper foreign policy is possible without forces and military alliances into which they can be fitted. Policy must be conducted if possible so that war never happens, but the means of waging it must remain in being and be strong enough to ensure that armed neighbours will prefer peace to the risk of defeat.

With the rise of modern technology the maintenance of such a service even at rest is costly because its weapons must be kept up to date by experiment and replacement. Beefeaters are not enough. Unfortunately it is the nature of an armed service designed for destructive ends to be unproductive. Thus the pursuit of foreign policy means that a part of the national resources of every country is 'standing by' and deliberately producing nothing useful. This is the background of the constant efforts, much impeded by mutual suspicion, to bring about some measure at least of world wide disarmament. It is not that disarmament will prevent wars, for it will not, but it will make peace more fruitful.

Space rocketry occupies an equivocal position in military affairs. Ostensibly designed for astronomical and other scientific research, the constant improvement of these missiles is obviously a terrible warlike threat. Yet their competitive use in the space race by the rival political camps distracts the world from their military aspect and, like the chariot races of Byzantium, lowers the political tensions by sublimating them. This, perhaps, is the justification for the vast diversion of industrial resources to these programmes which might otherwise be regarded as a scientist's racket of small value to the human race in comparison with the efforts required.

Diplomacy

The Foreign Service now comprises the former Diplomatic and Consular Services and the staffs under the Commonwealth Relations Office, but the detailed conduct of policy is shared between the latter and the Foreign Office so that an unitary service deals with two departments. Nowadays, however, the policy issues are settled increasingly by the Cabinet and their execution supervised by the Prime Minister. The two Secretaries of State have therefore declined notably in prestige.

This concentration perhaps reflects the specialist atmosphere in which foreign affairs are apt to be conducted. Apart from the experts and a few interested politicians only a small minority (mostly industrialists and bankers) of The 5000 exert their influence in relation to them or know much about it. It is perhaps for this reason, as much as any other, that balance of payments crises and similar economic difficulties tend to take the country by surprise.

There are United Kingdom missions abroad and overseas missions here. The British and overseas missions are all connected with their respective capitals by wireless and there is a constant traffic of ciphered messages; thus the foreign service requires not only diplomats and their necessary clerical staff but (since cipher causes delay) an army of radio operators and cipher clerks. This has revolutionized the technique and standing of diplomacy: formerly an ambassador negotiated with the government to whom he was accredited on the basis of standing instructions and his local knowledge, and used his comprehension of all the factors to bring about results for which (depending on his distance from home) he would be in a measure responsible. This is no longer the case; he can, and is expected to consult and report to his capital regularly and sometimes daily. He is told what to say; and his financial discretion is limited to fairly small sums. The representative side of the diplomat's function is withering away and is being replaced by those international meetings of politicians and 'summit meetings' so beloved by newspapers: and this is scarcely surprising, for the political head can fly there almost as quickly as his instructions can be written, enciphered, transmitted, deciphered and communicated.

The major function of a modern diplomatic mission is thus to gather all local information which will help the foreign policy of its own country, and to act as a post office for intergovernmental communications. It is also supposed to create a favourable image of its own country by good press relations and by cultural and other forms of propaganda, but few missions of any country anywhere seem to make much impression by these means.

One consequence of the centralization of direction is the rise of the diplomatic bureaucracy. The foreign offices of all major countries have expanded into great blocks of buildings where a few rooms only were thought necessary two generations ago.

But if diplomatic missions are ceasing to matter much, diplomacy itself is not. The need to discuss, to bargain and to agree is more urgently present every year as the world's populations and their means of self destruction increase. This need is being fulfilled more and more by international congresses and conferences and by the rise of international secretariats such as the United Nations Organization at New York, the Food and Agriculture Organizations at Rome, the Common Market Secretariat in Brussels, and the Council of Europe at Strasbourg.

Propaganda and Communication

The world is divided between the Communist and non-Communist alliances and the numerous uncommitted nations of Africa and Asia. The growing world horror at the apocalyptic probabilities of atomic war have led the rival armed camps to confine military operations to limited conventional wars and to wrestle for the souls of men. Wireless, television, Press, literature and travel exchange ideas and impressions between the nations. The average Russian no longer believes that Western man is an ogre, and Westerners are less certain than they were of the ill will of Communism. Each in fact is beginning to have doubts about the ill faith and aggressive determination of the other. The man with the gun may be less willing to pull the trigger when told: his master less willing to tell him. If this process is a two way traffic and continues for long enough a point may be reached where propaganda merges perceptibly into education. A mutual retreat from extreme positions might then become possible as between the West and Russia which is, after all, a European country with a European language and background. With the Chinese the situation is different. Their culture and language are their own: they do not and, because of the nature of their language, probably cannot use a phonetic alphabet without breaking up the unity of Chinese civilization. The chances of understanding with the rest of the world are therefore much less.

Thus propaganda occupies an international position somewhere between arms and diplomacy. Its object is not conquest or agreement but conversion. Its main target is the ruling groups which here consist of The 5000. Its time scale is a compromise, not expecting the hoped for quick results of war or resigned to the long periods of negotiation. The publicist, in other words, has superseded neither the soldier nor the negotiator; in the long run he may be more effective than either, but on condition that he really has something to say. A way of life cannot be supported upon a lie or a meaningless doctrine: the ably directed outpourings of the Axis propaganda machines were unable to conceal the fact that their Nazi and Fascist authors had not a single political ideal of any kind.

19

INTERNATIONAL TRENDS

The Decline of National Sovereignty

It never was possible for governments to behave as if other governments did not exist, but the condition of the modern world has placed new restrictions on the international freedom of all governments. These arise from the increasing complexity of physical civilization, the rapid growth of populations, and modern improvements in transport and transmission. To maintain high standards requires worldwide travel and commodity and commercial movements because no country can do this entirely from its own resources; gratuitous interruptions in the pattern of trade are likely to bring quick and disagreeable retaliation without necessarily leading to war.

On a more positive side some international dangers are being recognized by governments as threats to be combated in common. An aeroplane can bring a disease from a country with a resistant population to one whose population is vulnerable. Locusts know nothing of political frontiers. Famine destroys a market as surely as civil war. Illiteracy prevents industrial development. It is not enough to try and deal with individual cases as they come to notice because by the time the necessary special machinery has been set up the situation may be out of hand. And so permanent international agencies are growing up mostly under the patronage of the United Nations, and these are staffed by international servants responsible to the world at large and not to the country of their birth. If the United Nations cannot yet be a completely successful war-preventing machine, it already forestalls some disasters which could be equally damaging. Moreover it creates a habit of international co-operation which could spread to other fields and also engenders vested interests in the continuance of the organizations which then become difficult to dissolve. Most of all perhaps it maintains the image and hope of international government, by maintaining permanent institutions visibly resembling governmental departments.

The war preventing operations of the United Nations Organization have however not been wholly without success as Korea, the Congo and Sinai (for example) prove; and these have an interesting characteristic of their own. Once involved in a violent situation the Organization has found it in practice impossible to withdraw. As it has no peace-keeping forces of its own it has to use troops of disengaged (and usually smaller) member nations. In this way lesser powers like Sweden and Ethiopia are being involved directly in high world politics where otherwise they would have no influence.

International Powers

Under modern conditions there are a few powers whose behaviour can destroy the human race, but equally, international organization has reached a stage where many lesser nations are permanently inhibited from warlike action. Disturbances catch the headlines so readily that it is easy to forget that most of the thousands of miles of international frontiers are at peace and likely so to remain. The creation of new federal states such as a European Union, inevitable though it probably is, cannot be regarded without apprehension for it adds to the short list of powers capable of waging apocalyptic war. The profitable solution of this problem will be one of the major tasks of statesmanship in the next half century.

Part Five

RECAPITULATION
AND CONCLUSION

20

POLICY AND BALANCE

The greatest English constitutional problem is the reconciliation of individual dignity and rights with public requirements. It is the essence of our system that the electors are people who must be respected. Majority rule must, therefore, have regard for the interests of minorities, and the more important an interest to an individual the smaller the minority which qualifies for toleration. We still will not stand the unlawful imprisonment of a *single person* however objectionable, and in wartime we have arranged not to force the consciences of a *very small number of* honest pacifists. Rightly or wrongly the idea that a minority may be ruthlessly suppressed simply because its numbers are small is still repugnant to us.

This tolerant attitude is likely to remain only so long as the membership of The 5000 remains diverse.

But politics deals with the possible and the probable. It is not enough to make rules if they command insufficient obedience, and the use of force is expensive and creates problems of its own. A majority, ruthlessly led, can become a monstrous tyrant and can change the law to suit itself. Thus any country which intends to be governed according to principles must find means to establish the power of those principles over long periods of time. The essence of law is a degree of permanence. If Sunday's law could be changed on Monday and changed back on Tuesday nobody would recognize our system as a rule of law. It is not playing the game to change the rules in the middle of the match.

Perhaps by instinct, more probably by design, the many generations of minds which have shaped our system have seized

149

upon the time element and made it a vital part, if not the lynch-pin of the constitution. The ability of a government to govern depends upon public assent expressed through many political, non-political and journalistic channels, but its constitutional power to make changes is subject to the principle of time rationing which forces the party in power to choose between different elements in its policy and to place them in an order of priority. The fact that each change proposed will take time enables those to be affected to make their views known and their influence felt by such means as are available to them; it signifies, however, more than that: protraction of proceedings in Parliament and politics on one measure may compel a government to abandon some desired policy later in the queue and the fear of this possibility virtually compels governments to consult interested parties before a particular course is adopted.

It is often argued that this slow method is inefficient in that new situations are met too late and opportunities are lost. Viewed from a purely administrative point this is true, but it is not the purpose of the system to please administrators (rather the converse) and bad or dictatorial government will only be made worse by efficiency. Sudden and far-reaching changes carry with them their own peculiar brand of inefficiency: valuable things may be needlessly destroyed in securing the advantages sought. This comes out clearest in revolutions: the bloodshed and destruction are the price of too much haste. The civil wars and commotions of the 17th Century cost more than the nation has been willing to pay since. Recent attempts to tamper with parliamentary processes so as to speed them up, may have dangerous results.

Once peaceful change is accepted as the basis of political behaviour a second factor of great importance appears. The party in power knows in its heart of hearts that its rule will not last for ever and that another party will undo such of its work as cannot command the general and long term assent of the people. Policy will, therefore, be directed towards securing such assent and will be presented in a manner designed for that purpose. The existence of a well-organized opposition will in the long run make it impossible to cover up the true purposes of the government with lies – as happened in Hitler's Germany. There is thus a strong incentive to uphold a system which by its delays gives time for public debate and private consultation.

There is no aspect of life with which politics and government are not at some time concerned. There are laws about shopping hours and marriage, the maintenance of bridges and the protection of official secrets. The interests concerned in politics exist side by side and their representatives are found among The 5000; sometimes they are in opposition, at others indifferent or in alliance or overlapping, and these relationships change with time and circumstance. If building resources are short any encouragement to the motor industry might create a demand for new roads, which could in turn lower the rate of housebuilding. There may, therefore, be a conflict between motor and oil interests (and their many employees) and that portion of the public needing new houses, but both sides might agree on measures to increase building resources as a whole. Thus a motor-minded government might adopt the apparent compromise of favouring the builders. The state of deadlock amongst competing interests leads to a search for new solutions.

Moreover, governmental measures always have side effects which must be foreseen. To prohibit a dangerous type of domestic heater may not be enough: the innocent workers in the factory may be thrown on the street and if other manufacturers cannot increase production some people will go cold in the ensuing winter.

Thus a constitution must be so arranged that every facet of the national life is or can be reflected in it by some suitable means. This is not something which can be arranged neatly and defined in a document: it must be allowed to grow naturally, and at the centre there must be some place where any call will bring forth an echo. When the response is mute there is something wrong.

151

Cases of additions to the composition of The 5000 have been cited elsewhere. This is the most important way of keeping the centre in tune with the rest, but the decline of national sovereignty poses the question whether foreigners of various kinds such as the representatives of international banks, of certain great powers and of the United Nations have entered the circle. There have been several periods in our history when foreign ambassadors have been exceedingly powerful, and there is no reason why this should not happen again. This is quite unobjectionable if it is in the interests of the general welfare of the world.

In a previous chapter the proceedings on a bill in Parliament were briefly described. What any procedural narrative always lacks is the life which is lived between and before the legislative stages. A major policy will be initiated in pursuance of a direct or supposed mandate from the electors; the majority party, having formed a government, will deploy the resources of the civil service to turn the idea first into memoranda setting out the principles and tracing the probable effects, and then into public declarations of policy embodied in White Papers. By this time party exuberance will have simmered down and after the debates on the White Papers there will be instructions for legal draftsmen to frame a bill. The Ministry mainly involved will have to consult other ministries affected and very often outside bodies as well; there will be several confidential prints of the draft before the proposal is finally published in a legislative shape noticeably different from that which the earnest party workers probably expected.

At publication it will come under the scrutiny of bodies not hitherto consulted or left unsatisfied and they will approach members of the Houses and try to persuade them to champion their point of view. At these times shoals of letters pour into the parliamentary post office and there will be a constant stream of visitors and delegations.

This process of lobbying, discussion, drafting and correspondence goes on between all the many stages through which the bill goes. Theoretically it could create such pressure as to make an M.P.'s life intolerable and hold up business in the Houses indefinitely. In practice governments impose the Whip to settle a timetable; there is no constitutional safeguard against abuse of timetable motions except the knowledge that similar treatment will probably be accorded to the perpetrators when they are out of power. Governments find it hard after a November opening to get a major bill through before Easter, and the course of a private member without a whip to support him is even harder. There are all sorts of ways in which his bill can be obstructed short of an adverse vote so that every possible interest will have to be satisfied before it is published. This process of 'squaring everyone' can be extremely arduous even on a minor matter and so private members' bills are seldom long. Probably the most important in the 20th Century was Sir Alan Herbert's Matrimonial Causes Act and this had to be rescued by the government. The Parish Councils Bill, a minor measure, was filibustered in one session and almost fell victim to filibustering on a different bill in the next.

A visit to a centre of government can be illuminating. By the Thames stands the Royal Palace of Westminster whose site has long been given over to parliamentary institutions; alongside it is the Abbey, the coronation place of nine centuries of sovereigns.

In one half of the palace, dominated by the most famous clock in the world, is the debating Chamber of the House of Commons. Destroyed in the Second World War it has been rebuilt with all modern contrivances to ensure comfort and audibility. The seats are arranged in two blocks facing each other so that the distinction between government and opposition is emphasized; intentionally the chamber is not big enough to hold all the members, but is of such a size that mob oratory is impracticable. The Speaker (who has a palace of his own within the palace) occupies a splendid canopied chair at one end and behind him against the wall is a pew for silent civil servants. At the other end is a similar but less conspicuous pew

153

for private persons with a special interest in the business in hand.

Above the floor are galleries for diplomats, for peers, for the numerous and important Press and for the public who can obtain admission through their own member. Around and under the chamber is a honeycomb of lobbies and rooms where members talk, write letters and meet constituents, and the whole is completed by committee-rooms, bars and canteens. Thus this part of the building is dedicated to the public transaction of business by the public representatives.

In the middle of the palace is an ornate octagonal chamber surmounted by a spire. This is a sort of crossroads common to both Houses and called the Central Lobby and it is the place where ordinary people come to meet a member. It echoes all day with footsteps and conversation.

At the other end is the recently rebuilt Victoria Tower, a huge pile which contains the Sovereign's entrance and a great library in which all the parliamentary records are stored. The Lords' chamber is as it was built a century ago. The Throne stands empty except at the Opening, and in front of it is a curious sofa called the Woolsack upon which the Lord Chancellor sits. At the Bar there is a small pen for barristers arguing cases when the House is sitting judicially. The seating arrangements resemble those in the Commons, but there are fewer seats and more cross benches for peers who prefer not to be identified with a party. The atmosphere is one of intimate splendour. This part is obviously dedicated to the discussion of affairs by persons of distinction.

The Palace also contains many other places which in their way symbolize the nation's business. Ministers and Law Lords have their own rooms; there are typists' pools and even a typing agency; there are staffs of clerks, reference libraries and reading-rooms. There is a chapel and a barristers' robing-room. Thus party politics, religion, impartial discussion, law, the Press, the public, history, learning, ceremonial and the machinery of administration all have their place in one building; nevertheless outside in the streets and squares nearby – and sometimes far off – are buildings much larger in size and certainly more modern, and these are filled with civil servants.

The Speed of Change

A nation is never static, but on the other hand it can adapt itself to change only at a limited rate. The same is true of its constitution, the main use of which is to provide a means for keeping change at a rate which the ordinary people can stomach. Change must be neither too fast nor too slow. In the last few years there have been signs in this country that all is not well: the British constitution has been wrenched into shapes which earlier generations would find difficult to recognize.

Where formerly Britain was the admiration of the foreigner because of its freedom from regulation and bureaucracy, now it is difficult to get through a day without committing an offence or to do anything important without asking somebody else. Simultaneously, perhaps in reaction, there is a spirit of lawlessness quite as much in the way politicians daily change the law to suit themselves as in criminals who defy it. The victims are the same: namely the solid citizens who out of decency but to their disadvantage obey unforceable rules or rules in which they trust too much.

Law must contain elements of permanence and morality; but the necessity to equate the government's wishes with the moral order require more self-control than most governments possess; and while gross breaches of accepted morality, such as murder, are more lightly treated heavier and heavier penalties are imposed on those who contravene ephemeral government regulations. As a result a spirit of defiance and contempt seems to be rising between the governors and the governed; the political system is becoming overheated.

This is no opposition bogey (for the Conservative Party has done little to justify its name) but a simple question of human abilities. The speed of change seems faster than the ordinary man can comprehend and accept.

Part Six

APPENDICES

ACKNOWLEDGMENTS

The author acknowledges with thanks permission to print documents in Appendix I given respectively by the Comptroller of H.M. Stationery Office, the Kesteven County Council and the Chief Whip of the Conservative Party.

I: SOME PUBLIC DOCUMENTS

The following very small selection of public documents is printed here to illustrate both the working and the history of our institutions. Such documents are apt to perpetuate the spirit in which they were first drafted, even though they continue to be used for a modern purpose; for instance, the accession proclamation still echoes a period when the law of succession was not wholly free from doubt, and the new monarch's rights might have to be supported by the openly expressed consent of the most influential people available at the moment of change. Similarly the parliamentary proclamation recalls by the descriptive terms used for members of the House of Commons that England and Scotland once had separate parliaments.

1. *Accession Proclamation*

'Whereas it hath pleased Almighty God to call to his Mercy our late Sovereign Lord King George the Sixth of Blessed and Glorious Memory by whose Decease the Crown is solely and rightfully come to the High and Mighty Princess Elizabeth Alexandra Mary: We, therefore, the Lords Spiritual and Temporal of this Realm being here assisted with these of his late Majesty's Privy Council, with representatives of other members of the Commonwealth, with other principal Gentlemen of Quality, with the Lord Mayor, Aldermen and Citizens of the City of London do now hereby with one voice and Consent of Tongue and Heart publish and proclaim that the High and Mighty Princess Elizabeth Alexandra Mary is now by the death of our late Sovereign of Happy Memory become Queen Elizabeth the Second by the Grace of God Queen of this Realm and of all her other Realms

159

and Territories, Head of the Commonwealth, Defender of the Faith, to whom her Lieges do acknowledge all Faith and Constant Obedience with hearty and humble Affection; beseeching God by whom Kings and Queens do reign to bless the Royal Princess Elizabeth the Second with long and happy Years to reign over us.

Given at St. James's Palace this sixth day of February in the year of our Lord one thousand nine hundred and fifty-two.'
Here follow 191 signatures including those of Ministers, Judges of Appeal, City Aldermen and High Commissioners of Commonwealth countries.

2. *Proclamation to Dissolve a Parliament and Call Another*

ELIZABETH R.

Whereas we have thought fit by and with the advice of Our Privy Council to dissolve this present Parliament which stands prorogued to Tuesday, 10th May instant; We do, for that End publish this Our Royal Proclamation and do hereby dissolve the said Parliament accordingly: and the Lords Spiritual and Temporal and the Knights, Citizens and Burgesses and the Commissioners for Shires and Burghs of the House of Commons are discharged from their meeting and attendance on the said Tuesday, 10th May instant: And we being desirous and resolved as soon as may be to meet Our People and to have their Advice in Parliament do hereby make known Our Will and Pleasure to call a new Parliament: And do hereby further declare that by and with the Advice of our Privy Council, We have given Order that Our Chancellor of Great Britain and our Governor of Northern Ireland do respectively upon Notice thereof forthwith issue out writs in due form and according to Law for calling a New Parliament: and We do hereby also, by this our Proclamation under Our Great Seal of our Realm require writs forthwith to be issued accordingly by our said Chancellor and Governor respectively, for causing the Lords Spiritual and Temporal and Commons who are to serve in the said Parliament to be duly returned to and give their Attendance in Our said Parliament on Tuesday, 7th June next, which writs are to be returnable in due course of Law.

Given at Our Court at Buckingham Palace this 6th day of May in the year of Our Lord 1955 and in the fourth year of our reign.
God Save the Queen.

3. *Order in Council*

AT THE COURT AT BUCKINGHAM PALACE

The 6th Day of May 1955

Present,

THE QUEEN'S MOST EXCELLENT MAJESTY IN COUNCIL

Her Majesty having been this day pleased by Her Royal Proclamation to dissolve the present Parliament and to declare the calling of another is hereby further pleased by and with the advice of Her Privy Council to Order that the Lord High Chancellor of Great Britain and the Governor of Northern Ireland do respectively upon the notice of this Her Majesty's Order forthwith cause writs to be issued in due form and according to Law for the calling of a new Parliament to meet at the City of Westminster on Tuesday, 7th June, 1955; which writs are to be returnable in due course of Law.

W. G. Agnew.

4. *Writ of Habeas Corpus ad Subjiciendum*

Elizabeth the Second by the grace of God of the United Kingdom of Great Britain and Northern Ireland and of Our Other Realms and Territories, Queen, Head of the Commonwealth, Defender of the Faith:

To the Sheriff of Nottinghamshire greeting:

We command you that you have in the Queen's Bench Division of our High Court of Justice at the Royal Courts of Justice, London, immediately on receipt of this our writ the body of John Smith being taken and detained under your custody, as is said, together with the day and cause of his being taken and detained by whatsoever name he may be called therein, to undergo and receive all and singular such matters and things as our Court shall then and there consider of concerning him in this behalf: and have you there then this our writ.

Witness .... Lord Chief Justice of England at the Royal Courts of Justice, London the .... day of .... 19.....

161

5. *Bill and Act*

The following is a bill. If it were passed and became an Act it would be in exactly the same form except that the words 'A bill entituled' would be omitted.

Representation of the People Act 1949
Amendment

A

BILL

ENTITULED AN ACT
TO

Enable the wives of persons, who are employed abroad and prevented by the nature of their occupation from going in person to a polling station, to vote as absent voters in parliamentary elections.

BE IT ENACTED by the Queen's most Excellent Majesty, by and with the advice and consent of the Lords Spiritual and Temporal, and Commons, in this present Parliament assembled, and by the authority of the same, as follows:—

1. In section 12 of the Representation of the People Act, 1949, at the end of paragraph (*b*)(i) of subsection (1), and after the word "employment" in paragraph (*a*) of subsection (3), there shall be inserted the words 'or, in the case of a wife accompanying her husband abroad, the general nature of her husband's occupation, service or employment'.

2. This Act may be cited as the Representation of the People Act 1949 (Amendment) Act 1964.

[Bill 47]   43/1

6. *Statutory Instrument in Draft*

The following is the form of a draft statutory instrument ready to be laid before Parliament. If approved the final form would be the same except that the italicized note at the top would disappear as also the word DRAFT. In addition, a number would be inserted after 1963 and exact dates of making and coming into operation. The exact dates of signature by the Chief Registrar and the Lords Commissioners together with their names would also be printed.

Draft Order laid before Parliament under the Building Societies Act, 1960, s.1(8) and the Building Societies Act, 1962, s.21(6), for approval by resolution of each House of Parliament.

DRAFT STATUTORY INSTRUMENTS

1963 No.

BUILDING SOCIETIES

The Building Societies (Special Advances) Order 1963

Laid before Parliament in draft
Made   –   –   –   1963
Coming into Operation   1963

Whereas a draft of the following Order has been approved by a resolution of each House of Parliament as required by section 1(8) of the Building Societies Act, 1960(a) and section 21(6) of the Building Societies Act, 1962(b);

Now, therefore, the Chief Registrar, with the consent of the Treasury, pursuant to the powers conferred upon him by section 1(8) of the Building Societies Act, 1960 and section 21(4) of the Building Societies Act, 1962, and to all other powers enabling him in that behalf, hereby makes the following Order:—

1.—(1) This Order may be cited as the Building Societies (Special Advances) Order 1963, and shall come into operation on the day on which it is made.

(2) The Interpretation Act 1889(c) shall apply to the interpretation of this Order as it applies to the interpretation of an Act of Parliament.

2. The sum prescribed under section 1 of the Building Societies Act, 1960 and section 21 of the Building Societies Act 1962 shall, in relation to advances made by building societies in any financial year beginning on or after the date of the coming into operation of this Order, be seven thousand pounds.

Dated   1963.

Chief Registrar of Friendly
Societies.

We consent to this Order

Dated   1963.

Two of the Lords Commissioners
of Her Majesty's Treasury.

(a) 8 & 9 Eliz. 2.c.64 (b) 10 & 11 Eliz. 2.c.37. (c) 52 & 53 Vict. c.63.

EXPLANATORY NOTE

(This note is not part of the Order but is intended to indicate its general purport.)

This Order enables a building society to advance to an individual person £7,000 instead of £5,000 without the advance being treated as a special advance under the Building Societies Act, 1962, or (in the case of an unincorporated building society certified under the Building Societies Act, 1836) under the Building Societies Act, 1960.

7. *Warrant for a Royal Commission*

THE ROYAL WARRANT

ELIZABETH R.

ELIZABETH THE SECOND, by the Grace of God of the United Kingdom of Great Britain and Northern Ireland and of Our other Realms and Territories QUEEN, Head of the Commonwealth, Defender of the Faith, To

Our Trusty and Well-beloved:

Sir William Ivor Jennings, Knight Commander of Our Most Excellent Order of the British Empire, one of Our Counsel learned in the Law, Master of Arts, Doctor of Laws, Doctor of Letters;

164

Sir George Lionel Pepler, Knight, Companion of Our Most Honourable Order of the Bath, Past President of the Town Planning Institute, Fellow of the Royal Institution of Chartered Surveyors;

Sir Robert Donald Scott, Knight;

Laurence Dudley Stamp, Esquire, Commander of Our Most Excellent Order of the British Empire, Doctor of Science, Doctor of Letters, Professor of Social Geography, University of London;

Trevor George Corry Evans, Esquire, Officer of Our Most Excellent Order of the British Empire, Fellow of the Land Agents' Society;

Charles Murray Floyd, Esquire, Officer of Our Most Excellent Order of the British Empire, Fellow of the Land Agents' Society;

Charles Arnold-Baker, Esquire;

William George Hoskins, Esquire, Doctor of Philosophy;

Alan Lubbock, Esquire, Fellow of the Society of Antiquaries;

Ivor Raymond Morris, Esquire;

Florence Beatrice Paton, and

Robert Alun Roberts, Esquire, Doctor of Philosophy, Professor of Agricultural Botany, University College of North Wales, Bangor,

Greeting!

WHEREAS We have deemed it expedient that a Commission should forthwith issue to recommend what changes, if any, are desirable in the law relating to common land in order to promote the benefit of those holding manorial and common rights, the enjoyment of the public, or, where at present little or no use is made of such land, its use for some other desirable purpose:

NOW KNOW YE that We, reposing great trust and confidence in your knowledge and ability, have authorized and appointed, and do by these Presents authorize and appoint you the said Sir William Ivor Jennings (Chairman); Sir George Lionel Pepler; Sir Robert Donald Scott; Laurence Dudley Stamp; Trevor George Corry Evans; Charles Murray Floyd; Charles Arnold-Baker; William George Hoskins; Alan Lubbock; Ivor Raymond Morris; Florence Beatrice Paton and Robert Alun Roberts to be Our Commissioners for the purposes of the said inquiry:

AND for the better effecting the purposes of this Our Commission, We do by these Presents give and grant unto you, or

165

any four or more of you, full power to call before you such persons as you shall judge likely to afford you any information upon the subject of this Our Commission; to call for information in writing; and also to call for, have access to and examine all such books, documents, registers and records as may afford you the fullest information on the subject and to inquiry of and concerning the premises by all other lawful ways and means whatsoever;

AND We do by these Presents authorize and empower you, or any of you, to visit and personally inspect such places as you may deem it expedient so to inspect for the more effectual carrying out of the purposes aforesaid;

AND We do by these Presents will and ordain that this Our Commission shall continue in full force and virtue, and that you, Our said Commissioners, or any four or more of you may from time to time proceed in the execution thereof, and of every matter and thing therein contained, although the same be not continued from time to time by adjournment:

AND We do further ordain that you, or any four or more of you, have liberty to report your proceedings under this Our Commission from time to time if you shall judge it expedient so to do:

AND Our further will and pleasure is that you do, with as little delay as possible, report to Us your opinion upon the matters herein submitted for your consideration.

GIVEN at Our Court at Saint James's
in First day of December, 1955;
In the Fourth Year of Our Reign.
By Her Majesty's Command.
(Signed) G. LLOYD GEORGE.

8. *Byelaw*

COUNTY OF LINCOLN – PARTS OF KESTEVEN

Byelaw

for the good rule and government of the County of Lincoln, Parts of Kesteven, and for the prevention of nuisances, made by the Council of the County in pursuance of Section 249 of the Local Government Act, 1933, at a meeting of the Council held on the 19th day of November, 1952.

Carrying of Mud, Soil, etc., on to Highways

(1) A person in charge of a vehicle which is upon a highway shall, when to his knowledge any mud, clay, lime, or similar material has fallen on the highway from the vehicle and is likely if not removed therefrom to cause obstruction or danger to persons using the highway or injury to the surface of the highway, remove all such fallen material from the highway as completely as is reasonably practicable.

(2) Before a vehicle is brought upon a highway the person in charge of the vehicle shall as completely as is reasonably practical remove from the wheels thereof all mud, clay, lime and similar material which is likely if not so removed to cause obstruction or danger to persons using the highway or injury to the surface of the highway.

(3) If any sand or gravel which is or is about to be loaded into a vehicle for carriage along any highway, is saturated with water and the vehicle is not so constructed and maintained as to prevent the water dropping or leaking from it, any person in charge of the vehicle or the loading thereof shall take all such steps as are reasonably practicable to drain off the said water so that it shall not drop or leak from the vehicle on to the highway and render it dangerous to traffic.

(4) In this Byelaw:—

'highway' means a highway repairable by the inhabitants at large.
'vehicle' includes every machine or implement capable of carrying a load; and
'wheels' includes axles, runners and tracks.

Penalty

Every person who shall offend against the foregoing Byelaw shall be liable on summary conviction to a fine not exceeding Five Pounds for each offence.

Extent of Byelaw

This Byelaw shall extend and apply to all parts of the County of Lincoln, Parts of Kesteven, with the exception of the Municipal Boroughs of Grantham and Stamford.

GIVEN under the Common Seal of the County Council this nineteenth day of November, One thousand nine hundred and fifty-two.

THE Common Seal of the County Council of the Parts ⎫
of Kesteven was affixed hereto in pursuance of a ⎬
Resolution of the County Council. ⎭

(Sgnd) ROBERT PATTINSON
Chairman.

(Sgnd) J. E. BLOW
Clerk of the County Council.

I hereby confirm the foregoing Byelaw and fix the date on which it is to come into operation as 1st May, 1953.

(Sgnd) DAVID MAXWELL FYFE
One of Her Majesty's Principal
Secretaries of State.

Whitehall,
6th March, 1953.
32150–M

9. *A Whip*

The following is an example of the weekly whip which is sent by a chief whip to every member of his own party in the House of Commons. The wording and underlining are both important. As it happens this whip contains a reference to a free vote on one day. This being a party document it indicates to a member the importance attached by his party to the particular forthcoming events thus:

(1) a single line whip = either no division is expected or (as in this case) a division is not of much party significance;

(2) a two line whip = this is fairly important and a division is expected not too late at night.

(3) a three line whip = a division is certain and every member must be present unless unavoidably detained by illness.

On Monday, 27th October, 1947, the House will meet at 2-30 p.m.
    Continuation of the General debate on the Address.
    Discussion on Germany until 8-30 p.m., then
    Opposition Amendment on Imperial Security. (Mr.J.P.L.Thomas).
    Your attendance at 3-30 p.m. and throughout the Sitting

is requested. A division will take place at 11 p.m.

On Tuesday, 28th October, the House will meet at 2-30 p.m.
            Debate on the Address.
            Opposition Amendment.
    Your attendance at 3-30 p.m. and throughout the sitting

is requested.

On Wednesday, 29th October, the House will meet at 2-30 p.m.
    Conclusion of the debate on the Address.
            Opposition Amendment.
    Your attendance at 3-30 p.m. and throughout the Sitting is

particularly requested. A most important division or divisions

will take place.

On Thursday, 30th October, the House will meet at 2-30 p.m.
    Consideration of the Reports from the Committee of
Privileges relating to the cases of the Hon. Members for
Gravesend (Mr. Garry Allighan) and Doncaster (Mr. Evelyn Walkden).
    Your attendance at 3-30 p.m. and throughout the Sitting
is requested. There will be a free Vote of the House.

On Friday, 31st October, the House will meet at a.m.
    Expiring Laws Bill; Committee & remaining stages.
    Jersey and Guernsey (Financial Provisions) Bill; 2nd Reading.
    Motions to approve the Fish Sales (Charges) Order and the 4
    Purchase Tax Orders on the Paper.
    Your attendance at 11 a.m. and throughout the Sitting

is requested.

                          WILLIAM WHITELEY.

Note.
    During the week it is hoped to consider the Motion relating
to the Parliamentary Electors (War-Time Registration) Act, 1944.
    A Prayer has been tabled for consideration on Tuesday.

II: LIST OF IMPORTANT CONSTITUTIONAL EVENTS

602	Augustine first Archbishop of Canterbury
664	Synod of Whitby
710	The Laws of Ine
802	Egbert first King of all the English
871–899	Reign of Alfred the Great
1066	Norman Invasion
1069	Devastation of the North
1086	Domesday Book
1215	Magna Carta
1265	Simon de Montfort's Parliament
1295	Model Parliament
1297	Confirmatio Cartarum
1381	Wat Tyler's Revolt
1455–71	Wars of the Roses
1485	Henry VII King
1534	Act of Supremacy confirms separation of the Anglican Church from Rome
1536–40	Dissolution of the Monasteries
1600	Elizabethan Poor Law establishes the Rating System
1603	James VI of Scotland becomes King of England as well
1628	Petition of Right
1634–9	The Ship Money Proceedings
1640	Long Parliament Begins
1641	Attainder of Strafford
	Abolition of Star Chamber and High Commission
1642	Beginning of the Civil War
1649	Charles I beheaded
1660	Restoration of Charles II
1688	Flight of James II
1689	Bill of Rights
1707	Union of England and Scotland
1712	Abandonment of anti-French policy against Lords opposition

170

1714	George I King
1721–42	Walpole's Ministry
1745–6	Scottish Rebellion and Abolition of Tribal Jurisdictions
1776	American Declaration of Independence
1783–1801	First Administration of William Pitt the Younger
1799	First Introduction of Income Tax
1800	Union of Britain and Ireland
1832	Reform Bill passes
1837	Victoria Queen
1875–1894	First Public Health Act, Creation of County Councils and other Councils
1911	Parliament Act
1913	Provisional Collection of Taxes Act 1913
1914–18	World War I
1918	Women over 30 enfranchised
1920	Welsh Church disestablished
1921	Southern Ireland independent
1929	Women between 21–30 enfranchised
1931	Statute of Westminster 1931
1939–45	World War II
1952	Finance Act, 1952. (Security for taxes payable solely under resolution of the Commons.)
1961	Finance Act, 1961. (Treasury power to vary customs and excise.)
1965	Rhodesian secession
1966	Second Wilson Administration, Introduction of morning sessions in the House of Commons

III: THE SIZE AND COMPOSITION OF GOVERNMENTS

The following lists of office holders in two governments nearly a century apart illustrate the way in which the composition of governments has changed and the number of paid offices available to politicians increased.

It is not possible to make exact equivalences in a table such as this. For instance the public status of the English Law Officers was much higher in 1868 than it is today, and the Lord Advocate performed in addition to his own most of the work now done by the Secretary of State for Scotland.

Moreover in 1868 there were several very high political offices such as the Lord Lieutenancy of Ireland which were 'of' the government but not 'in' it and which no longer exist, while nowadays there is a varying number of unpaid parliamentary private secretaries who did not exist in 1868.

1868 Gladstone's First Administration	*1966* Mr Wilson's Second Administration
(15) CABINET (23)	
Prime Minister and ⎱ First Lord of the Treasury ⎰	Prime Minister and ⎱ First Lord of the Treasury ⎰
Lord President of the Council	Lord President of the Council
Lord Chancellor	Lord Chancellor
Chancellor of the Exchequer	Chancellor of the Exchequer
Lord Privy Seal	Lord Privy Seal
	First Secretary of State and ⎱ Secretary for Economic ⎰ Affairs

172

1868	*1966*

Secretaries of State for:

Home Department	Home Department
Foreign Affairs	Foreign Affairs
War (i.e. Army only)	Defence (i.e. all Services)
Colonies	Colonies
India	—
—	Education and Science
—	Commonwealth Relations
—	Scotland
—	Wales
Chief Secretary for Ireland	—
First Lord of the Admiralty	—
President of the Poor Law Board	—
President of the Board of Trade	President of the Board of Trade
Postmaster General	—
—	Minister of Overseas Development
—	Minister of Housing and Local Government
—	Minister of Labour
—	Minister of Technology
—	Minister of Agriculture, Fisheries & Food
—	Minister of Power
—	Minister of Transport
—	Minister without Portfolio

(5)	MINISTERS NOT IN THE CABINET:	(28)
—	Postmaster General	

Ministers:

—	Health
—	Pensions and National Insurance
Commissioner of Works	Public Building and Works
—	Aviation
—	Land and Natural Resources
—	Without Portfolio
Paymaster-General	Paymaster-General
—	Chief Secretary to the Treasury

173

1868	*1966*

Ministers of Defence:

—	Royal Navy
—	Royal Air Force
—	Army

Ministers of State:

President of the Board of Education	⎧ Education and Science ⎨ Education and Science ⎩
—	⎧ Foreign Affairs
—	⎪ Foreign Affairs ⎬
—	⎪ Foreign Affairs
—	⎩ Foreign Affairs
—	Home Office
—	Commonwealth Relations
—	⎧ Board of Trade
Vice-President of the Board of Trade	⎨ Board of Trade
	⎩ Board of Trade
—	Scottish Office
—	Welsh Office
—	Economic Affairs
Chancellor of the Duchy of Lancaster	Chancellor of the Duchy of Lancaster

(4)	*Law Officers*	(2 + 2)

Attorney General	Attorney General
Solicitor General	Solicitor General
Lord Advocate	Lord Advocate*
Solicitor General for Scotland	Solicitor General for Scotland*
	* not in parliament

(15)	*Junior Ministers*	(55)

—		Agriculture	2
—		Aviation	1
Colonies	1	Colonies	1
—		Commonwealth Relations	1
Admiralty	1 ⎫	Defence	3
War Office	1 ⎭	—	
—		Economic Affairs	1
Education	1	Education and Science	2
Foreign Office	1	Foreign Office	1
—		Health	1
Home Office	1	Home Office	3

1868			1966	
—			Housing and Local Goverment	3
—			Land and Natural Resources	1
—			Labour	1
—			Overseas Development	1
—			Pensions and National Insurance	1
Post Office	1		Post Office	1
—			Power	1
Works			Public Building and Works	1
—			Scottish Office	3
—			Technology	2
—			Board of Trade	1
—			Transport	2
Treasury	5		Treasury	8
—			Other Whips in the Commons	8
—			Whips in the Lords	4
—			Welsh Office	1
	39	Totals		110

SHORT LIST OF BOOKS

ALLEN, SIR CARLETON, *Law and Orders*. Stevens, London, 1956, pp. 482.

CHESTER, D. N., *Central and Local Government*. Macmillan, London, 1951, pp. 421.

CROSS, C. A., *Local Government Law*. Sweet & Maxwell, London, 1962, pp. 465, plus index.

ERSKINE MAY'S PARLIAMENTARY PRACTICE. Butterworth, London, 1964, pp. 1,086, plus index.

JENNINGS, SIR IVOR, *Cabinet Government*. Cambridge University Press, 1959, pp. 570, plus index.

— *Parliament*. Cambridge University Press, 1957, pp. 548, plus index.

KEIR, SIR DAVID LINDSAY, *Constitutional History of Modern Britain since 1485*. A. & C. Black, London, 1966, pp. 569, plus index.

MACKENZIE, W. J. M., and GROVE, J. W., *Central Administration in Great Britain*, Longmans, London, 1957, pp. 487.

MORRISON, RT. HON. HERBERT (Lord Morrison of Lambeth), *Government and Parliament*. Oxford University Press, 1959, pp. 369, plus index.

GLOSSARY

A number of expressions are included which are not mentioned in the text.

Abdication (1) A demise of the Crown otherwise than by death; not now possible save by Act.

(2) In addition the following British sovereigns are considered to have abdicated: John Balliol of Scotland, 1296; Edward II, 1327; Richard II, 1399; Mary of Scots, 1567; James II, 1688.

Abeyance Certain old peerages in the absence of male heirs descend equally to sisters and their heirs (i.e. the younger has an equal right with the elder). A peerage being indivisible, it cannot be enjoyed or exercised until the different lines of heirs have been reduced to one by extinction. In the interval the peerage is said to be in abeyance. Abeyances have lasted for centuries.

'Abolition' See Slavery.

Absolutism Dictatorship by a monarch.

Abuse The use·of a statutory power for a purpose other than that for which it was created, or in a manner not contemplated by the law.

Act A law by the agreement of Crown, Lords and Commons in Parliament.

'Act of State' Something done by the government which cannot be challenged by proceedings in the courts. Limited under English Law to acts (such as acts of war) in the pursuit of foreign policy.

Act of Union 1707 The instruments which united England and Scotland.

Address Any message sent by a house of parliament to the Crown, especially the message of thanks for the terms of the Speech from the Throne.

Administration See Government.

Air Council A council of the highest air staff officers which under the chairmanship of the Minister for Defence (Air) administers the R.A.F.

Alderman (1) Except in the City of London, a person selected by the Councillors of a County or Borough to serve for six years. The proportion of such aldermen to councillors is one to three.

(2) In the City of London a person elected by the electors at large to represent his ward for life. The proportion of such aldermen to councilmen is less than one to six.

Alien. A person who is not a British Subject or Denizen and can be deported or refused admission.

Allegiance (1) The relationship between a subject and the Crown;
(2) The obligations to the Nation, breach of which is treason.

Allegiance, Oath of An oath or affirmation required as a prerequisite of service in certain offices, notably membership of Parliament and on naturalization.

Ambassador The highest ranking diplomatic representative of a foreign power.

Anarchism A view of society whose proponents regard government as an evil and who therefore prefer to have as little of it as possible (not to be confused with anarchy).

Arbitration (1) The settlement of disputes by an independent person and not by resort to the courts.

(2) The settlement on the merits of disputes between States by an independent person, other State or international court and not by negotiation, war, or other imposed solution.

Arbitration, International Court of A court set up at the Hague in 1901 to settle international disputes between countries who have either permanently or for the occasion submitted to its jurisdiction.

Army Council A council of the high military officers which, under the chairmanship of the Minister of Defence (Army) administers the Army.

Attainder, Act of A method of condemning a person to penalties (usually death) without trial by passing a bill through Parliament. A grossly unjust proceeding long since disused.

Attorney General The Government's Chief Law Officer and Legal Adviser. He is a politician.

Ballot The method of election by secret written vote.

Bar (1) A barrier across a House of Parliament marking the point at which non-members are turned back.

(2) A similar barrier across a law court marking the point within which only court officials and Q.C.s may go.

(3) That part of the legal profession consisting of barristers in England and advocates in Scotland.

Baronet A hereditary knight.

Big Ben The clock and its bell at the Palace of Westminster. Named after Sir Benjamin Hall, first commissioner of works; erected in 1856.

Bill A draft law (Act) before it has received the Royal Assent. A *public* bill is introduced by a member of one House or the other; a *private* bill is introduced through the medium of a petition from someone who is not a member; not to be confused with a private member's bill.

Black Rod, Gentleman Usher of the A court official who has for centuries been on permanent loan to the House of Lords to manage their administration.

Blue Book A collection of papers on a particular subject printed and bound for use by members of either House of Parliament.

Bow Street Colloquially the court of the Chief Metropolitan Magistrate. He alone has power to deal with applications for extradition.

Budget The plan of expenditure and revenue-raising annually submitted to the House of Commons sitting in Committee of the whole House.

Cabinet The committee of senior ministers which under the chairmanship of the Prime Minister decides the policy of the government.

Canon Law (1) The law of ecclesiastical matters.

(2) The law specially appertaining to the established churches.

Chancery (1) The Office of a chancellor.

(2) That part of the law which deals with property, trusts and the guardianship of children. (*See* p. 82–84.)

Charity A fund originating in private generosity applicable to certain public purposes such as education, relief of poverty, public recreation, religion etc.

Charity Commission The body exercising the administrative supervision of charities, other than educational charities which are supervised by the Department of Education and Science.

Charter A document issued by the Crown nowadays mainly to create and constitute a corporation. All boroughs and some companies (e.g. the Hudson's Bay Company) have charters.

Chequers The country residence of the Prime Minister.

Chiltern Hundreds The stewardship of these three hundreds together with that of Northstead are sinecures which in law are offices of profit under the Crown. A member of the House of Commons ceases to be a member if he accepts such an office. A member desiring to resign therefore applies for one of these offices, which can be refused. He can resign in no other way.

Chivalry, Court of A court which deals with heraldic disputes in England. It seldom sits.

Church Assembly The sublegislature dealing with affairs of the Church of England. It consists of Bishops, Clergy and Laity. (*See* Measure.)

Church of England The Anglican Episcopal branch of the universal church. It is established in England (except Monmouthshire). The Sovereign is its head on earth and its Archbishops and twenty-four of its bishops sit in the House of Lords.

Church of Scotland The Presbyterian established Church in Scotland.

Cinque Ports An ancient confederation in Kent and Sussex once of *five* ports (now seven) with other places formed for coast defence. Now largely ceremonial but its Lord Warden is usually a statesman of great distinction.

Citizen A person who actually or theoretically has rights in a particular country.

Civil Law (1) The basic non-statutory law of Scotland.

(2) That part of any system of law which deals with civil relationships as opposed to criminal activities.

Civil List The sum annually paid to the Sovereign in lieu of the much larger proceeds of the Crown Estate and hereditary revenues.

Civil Service The collection of permanent paid public servants who carry out the orders of the government.

Civil Wars It has been calculated that since 1066 about fifty-five years have been occupied with civil wars.

Closure A motion for ending a debate.

Coalition A government including supporters of more than one party.

Colony An overseas territory for whose administration the British Government is responsible.

Commission (1) A document issued by the Crown empowering someone to exercise certain functions, e.g. to a military officer or a judge.

(2) A person or more usually a committee of persons to whom a commission has been issued, e.g. to inquire into a matter of importance and make recommendations.

Comity A legal rule of growing importance that the courts will in certain civil disputes enforce foreign law.

Committee Stage The stage after Second Reading in legislation where the details of a bill are examined by either House.

Committee of Ways and Means A committee of the whole House of Commons (less the speaker) to consider the finance of a measure.

Committee of Supply A committee of the whole House of Commons to consider the granting of funds to carry on the government.

Common Council The lower Council of the City of London elected annually.

Common Law The basic non-statutory law of England and Wales, and Northern Ireland.

Commonwealth (1) The countries formerly or still subject to the British Crown and which still recognize a special relationship with the United Kingdom and obtain special advantages from that relationship. Burma and South Africa have left the Commonwealth.

(2) The period between the death of Charles I (1649) and the Restoration of Charles II (1660).

Commonwealth Conference A Meeting of Commonwealth Prime Ministers.

Commonwealth Secretariat A new intergovernmental organization now functioning at Marlborough House, London.

Comptroller and Auditor General An independent public official who has the oversight of all sums appropriated to and spent by Ministries, and through whom the Public Accounts are submitted to the Public Accounts Committee.

Conscription Compulsory service to the State usually but not invariably in the armed forces.

Consolidated Fund A fund from which certain payments (such as judges' salaries) are paid automatically each year under a statutory authority not confined to the annual budget.

Consolidation The technical term for the codification of statues by repeal and substantive re-enactment in a single act.

Consultative Council or Committee A body which has no executive functions or responsibilities but is entitled only to offer advice. Mainly found in nationalized industries.

Convention Parliament A parliament assembled without a summons from the Crown. Specifically the Parliament of 1660 which proclaimed the Restoration and that of 1689 which offered the Crown to William III and Mary II.

Convocation An assembly of the Bishops and Clergy of a Province, especially of Canterbury and York, whose Convocations were till 1966 dissolved and re-elected at the same time as Parliament.

Cornwall, Duchy of A group of rights and estates (mostly in the West Country) which vest automatically in the eldest son of the Sovereign.

Corporation (1) Any collection of people treated by the law as a single person or 'body corporate'.

(2) Colloquicially the council of a borough.

Councillor An elected member of a local authority.

Councilman A member of the Common Council of the City of London.

Court Martial A court of officers empowered to try members of the armed services for breaches of service law and discipline. In time of war outside British territory it may try them for breaches of ordinary criminal law as well.

Crime An act rendering the person who commits it liable to punishment.

Crown (1) The chief insignia of royalty worn on the head.

(2) The sovereign in the abstract.

Crown Estate The lands and properties belonging to the sovereign which are administered for the benefit of the Treasury by commissioners.

Curia Regis The medieval King's Court from which the Exchequer, the Law Courts, the House of Lords and the Privy Council developed.

Customs (1) Rules enforced by the courts because they are reasonable, of long standing, and easily defined and so may be assumed to be part of a 'local common law'.

(2) A tax levied at the point of entry upon goods brought from abroad.

(3) Anything done by habit.

Danegeld The earliest regular tax, originally levied in late Saxon times to finance government policy in relation to the Danish invasions.

Defender of the Faith A title used by all English sovereigns since 1521.

Demise of the Crown The passing of the Crown (by death or abdication) from one sovereign to another.

Department A ministry. More strictly a ministry headed by a Secretary of State.

Deposit £150 which a candidate must deposit with the returning officer in a parliamentary election and which is returned to him if he receives more than one eighth of the votes cast.

Development Commission A government department which disburses small sums annually to assist the development of rural areas.

Diplomat A public servant who specializes in the conduct of foreign affairs.

Disestablishment The conversion of a church from a public official body whose rules have the force of law into a private organization whose rules bind its members only as contracts. The Church of England is disestablished everywhere except in England (other than Monmouthshire), Isle of Man and the Channel Isles.

Dissolution The termination of a parliament's existence.

Dominion Discussed under Westminster, Statute of.

Downing Street (1) A small cul-de-sac off Whitehall. No. 10 is the official town house of the Prime Minister. No. 11 that of the Chancellor of the Exchequer.

(2) Used sometimes as a synonym for the Prime Minister.

Electors Those British subjects or Citizens of Ireland who have a right to vote in elections. They must be over twenty-one and have their name on the register of the area for which a given election is being held. The right to be registered depends on residence in the area on a qualifying date in the twelve months before the register comes into force.

Enabling Act (1) Any act which empowers a person or body to do something which legally it would otherwise be unable to do.

(2) More specifically the Act which confers legislative powers on the Church Assembly.

Estimates The statements of intended government expenditure which precede the introduction of the budget.

Exchequer A financial department of State originally concerned with receipt of taxes and issues of payments. (*See* Treasury.)

Excise A tax levied on goods originating in the United Kingdom.

Extradition The process of removing a person suspected of an offence against the laws of a foreign country to that country for trial. Extradition from the United Kingdom is only granted to a country with whom there is an extradition treaty covering the offence alleged and will not be enforced against a genuinely political refugee. Commonwealth countries are not foreign in this sense. (*See* Fugitive Offenders and Bow Street).

Fabian Society An intellectual society of non-revolutionary socialists influential in the Labour Party.

Filibuster To speak at unlimited length in order to obstruct the proceedings of a legislature.

Financial Resolution If a bill involves expenditure of public funds, it must originate in the House of Commons and after Second Reading it cannot proceed unless the relevant expenditure is authorized by a financial resolution moved by the Government in Committee of the whole House.

First Reading The formal first stage when a bill is introduced into a House of a Parliament. It is really a notice of intention.

Five Members Pym, Hampden, Hazelrigg, Strode and Holles, whom Charles I tried in person to arrest on 4 January 1642. No monarch has set foot in the Commons since then.

Floating Voter A voter whose opinions cannot be predicted.

Foreign Office The British Ministry of Foreign Affairs headed by a Secretary of State.

Franchise Now mainly the right to vote in an election.

Fugitive Offenders A person accused of an offence in one territory of the Commonwealth must be deported to that territory from any other for trial. Political considerations are irrelevant.

Gallup Poll Named after a Dr Gallup. A method of testing public opinion by questioning a very small sample. Political leaders tend to rely on Gallup Polls increasingly to help decide important issues.

General Assembly The name given to the respective sublegislatures of the Churches of England and Scotland.

Government (1) The collection of politicians occupying the 100 or so principal offices of state; the 'administration'.

(2) The politicians and civil servants collectively administering the country.

Guillotine A closure motion in the House of Commons laying down in advance the time when a debate on a given matter shall end.

Habeas Corpus A writ (i.e. a formal order) issued by a court requiring anyone who is detaining someone else to bring the latter before the court and explain under what authority he is detaining him.

Hansard The usual name for the verbatim report of proceedings in both Houses of Parliament. Originally compiled privately by a Mr Hansard.

High Commissioner The official representative of one commonwealth country at the capital of another (an Ambassador always represents a foreign State).

Honours The titles and decorations conferred by the Crown. They range from peerages to commendations and are mostly given on the recommendation of the Prime Minister, the Prime Ministers of certain Commonwealth States and the Secretaries of State for Defence, Foreign Affairs and Commonwealth Relations. The following apart from peerages are the main types of honour:

Granted by the Crown (*without recommendation*) *for public services or merit of the highest kind,*
    Knighthoods of the Garter and Thistle
    Order of Merit.

For personal service to the Sovereign,
    Victorian Order.

For high public service in a military, naval or civil capacity,
    Order of the Bath.

For public service abroad or as a diplomat,
    Order of St Michael and St George.

For services in the public interest but not necessarily in the service of the Crown,
    Order of the British Empire.

For Conspicuous Bravery,
    V.C. (Armed Services).

183

G.C. (Civilians).

Honours List The list of honours to be conferred. Published at the New Year, the Sovereign's Birthday, and on the resignation of a Prime Minister. (See Patronage.)

Impeachment A method of trial used only in the case of very high personages accused of conduct in office prejudicial to the safety of the state or injurious to the nation's interest. The charges are brought by the House of Commons and tried by the Lords. Disused since *1805*.

Inland Revenue The organization which collects taxes in the United Kingdom such as income tax, surtax, etc.

Inns of Court The four societies of barristers (the Inner Temple, Middle Temple, Lincoln's Inn and Gray's Inn).

Jury Twelve persons (fifteen in Scotland) chosen at random to try the issues of *fact* in serious cases before the courts.

Justice (1) 'The constant and perpetual desire to render to each his due'. (Justinian.)
(2) The law as enforced by courts.
(3) A judge of the High Court.

Justice of the Peace (*J.P.*) A lay unpaid magistrate appointed by the Lord Chancellor on the recommendation of a committee in each county.

Justiciar A medieval viceroy, prime minister or deputy for the King in the latter's absences.

Knighthood An honour conferred by the Crown entitling the holder to be addressed by his christian name with the prefix 'Sir'.

Labour Party The party with a socialist programme supported by the Trades Unions and headed by such figures as Lord Attlee, Mr Aneurin Bevan and Mr Harold Wilson. The moderate Left.

Land Registry A public office where the title to any land may be registered and where the title to land in certain places (such as London and Kent) *must* be registered. The area of compulsory registration is being slowly extended.

Law A body of rules which those whom they affect will be compelled impartially to obey by force.

Law Courts The commonly used name for the buildings of the Supreme Court of Justice in the Strand, London. It contains mainly civil courts.

Law Officers (1) In England the Attorney-General and Solicitor General.
(2) In Scotland the Lord Advocate and Solicitor General.

Left The body of political opinion which is generally dissatisfied with the existing state of affairs and advocates change. (*See* Right.)

Legislation (1) The process by which laws are made, especially the parliamentary process.
(2) Written (as opposed to customary) laws.

Legislature An assembly with power to make laws.

Letters Patent (1) A public or open ('patent') letter addressed by the Crown to a person or persons conferring a power, dignity, privilege or immunity. Commissions of Assize and peerages are granted by letters patent.

(2) Especially a right granted to an inventor to the exclusive exploitation of his invention for a period usually of fourteen years.

Liberal Party A radical party opposed both to the Conservatives and to Socialism.

Local Authority The council of a county, borough (or Scottish burgh), district or parish.

Local Government A term commonly used to mean the collection of locally elected councils which carry out some of the functions of local administration. (*See* p. 100.)

Lord (1) Peers, and members of the peerage of Ireland are Lords.

(2) The official title of a judge in Scotland.

Lord Chancellor A high dignatory who acts simultaneously as Speaker of the House of Lords, head of the judiciary and nowadays as Keeper of the Great Seal. He is always a member of the Cabinet.

Lord Lieutenant Originally a military officer appointed to command the shire levy. Nowadays the social and ceremonial head of a county with responsibilities connected with recommendations for honours and magistracies. He is always named as a commissioner of assize. (*See* p. 83.)

Lord Marcher A medieval border baron entitled to rule his territory without reference to the central government and to maintain a private military force.

Magna Carta An agreement on certain rules and liberties between King John and the barons made in 1215 in the form of a concession by the King and regularly renewed in the later Middle Ages.

Mandate The consent of the electors to the government's policy assumed from the fact that the government party stated its policy intentions at a general election, and the electors returned a majority of that party to the House of Commons.

Mansion House (1) The official residence of a number of Lord Mayors, especially the Lord Mayor of London.

(2) Used to represent the office of Lord Mayor of London especially in connection with charitable appeals.

Mayor Chairman of a borough council in England and Wales and Northern Ireland. Certain mayors are called 'Lord Mayor'.

Measure A law dealing with the affairs of the Church of England. It is passed by the Assembly of the Church of England and becomes law when approved by resolution of both Houses of Parliament. It has the force of an Act of Parliament.

Minister (1) The political head of any department of State.

(2) More accurately a high political servant of the Crown inferior in rank only to a Secretary of State.

185

(3) A diplomatic official ranking immediately below an Ambassador.

Mint The State coin factory. The Master of the Mint is the Chancellor of the Exchequer.

Money Bill A public bill dealing with taxation or expenditure and certified by the Speaker to be a money bill. Such a bill can be debated in the House of Lords who, however, have no power to alter or reject it.

Monopolies Except in the special case of patents (*see* Letters Patent) it is illegal for the Crown by itself to grant a private monopoly. The monopolies enjoyed by nationalized industries were created by Acts of Parliament.

National Debt The total amount of borrowed money at any given time in the hands of the Government, repayment of which is secured on the public revenue as a whole.

National Governments Coalitions which held power in Britain 1931–35 and 1939–46.

National Service Formerly compulsory service in the armed forces.

N.A.T.O. North Atlantic Treaty Organization.

Nationality The condition of belonging to a group of people subject to a particular sovereign State.

Natural Justice A name given to a rule that a person should always be given an opportunity of stating his case if someone else has been allowed to state a case against him.

Naturalization (1) The process whereby a foreigner becomes a British Subject.

(2) Any process whereby a person changes his nationality.

1922 Committee An influential committee of conservative parliamentary backbenchers.

Old Bailey The common name for the Central Criminal Court for Greater London.

Order in Council (1) See p. 79.

(2) Especially the orders enforcing the naval blockades of Europe in the Napoleonic Wars.

Parliament Acts 1911 and 1949 Acts which forbid the House of Lords from meddling with money bills and reduce its power of delay over other public bills to two consecutive sessions and one year. Very seldom used.

Partition The division of a country into more than one State, particularly the division of Ireland.

Pass Stage The stage in legislation where a House decides that its work on a bill is finished and it can be sent ('passed') elsewhere, i.e. as the case may be to the other House for consideration or to the Crown for Assent.

Patronage The power to confer honours and preferments. Now exercised by the Crown on the advice of the Prime Minister.

Peer Now a lay member of the House of Lords.

Petition of Right Presented to Charles I, 1627. Not to be confused with the Bill of Rights, 1689.

Plebiscite (1) A vote upon a particular issue by the electors of an area, intended to decide the issue independently of the wishes of a legislature or government.

(2) More often the choice made by the electors of certain border areas as to which country they wish to belong to.

Politician (1) A person actively engaged in party politics.

(2) Now a member of the House of Commons.

Prayer Some statutory instruments require to be confirmed by positive resolution of each House. Others come into force after forty days unless a motion 'praying' the Crown to withdraw the instrument is carried in one House or the other.

Prerogative The common law powers of the Crown.

Prime Minister The Crown's chief adviser and head of the government. He is the leader of a majority in the House of Commons. He is nowadays always First Lord of the Treasury.

Privilege The special rights of the Houses of Parliament.

Privy Council The most ancient council of Crown advisers. Its Judicial Committee acts as the supreme court of appeal from colonies and some other independent countries in the Commonwealth.

Privy Purse The office which deals with the Sovereign's private finances.

Privy Seal A seal formerly used for authenticating certain documents expressing the official wishes of the Crown on matters which were not of universal application, e.g. the management of an ancient crown manor. It was abolished long ago by Act of Parliament, but the high officer in charge of it (the Lord Privy Seal) still exists.

Probate That part of the law concerned with the proper execution of wills and their subsequent administration. (See p. 84.)

Prohibition (1) Laws forbidding the drinking of alcohol.

(2) A High Court procedure for prohibiting an inferior court from exceeding its jurisdiction.

Prorogation The Act by which the Crown brings a session of Parliament to an end.

Protectorate (1) An independent State which by treaty has accepted protection from another State more powerful than itself, usually in return for a surrender of control over its own foreign policy.

(2) The period when Oliver and Richard Cromwell held office as 'Lord Protector'.

Provost (1) Chairman of a Scottish Burgh Council. The more important ones are called 'Lord Provost'.

(2) The chairman of a new cathedral chapter in England.

Public Accounts Committee A committee of the House of Commons which scrutinises the financial dealings of ministries.

Public Trustee A public official who will act as trustee of private funds if requested to do so.

Public Works Loans Board A body for lending government funds to Local Authorities.

Queen When the sovereign is a King, his wife, though called the Queen, is his subject.

Question Time A daily period of about an hour (usually at the beginning of the day's proceedings) when members of either House (especially of the Commons) question ministers about matters for which they are responsible. Notice of questions must be given in advance, but 'supplementary questions' are allowed by word of mouth after the answer to the written question has been given. In addition many questions are answered in writing.

Rate A tax on property levied by local councils.

Realm A kingdom. Now tending to be used in official language to express the commonwealth countries which are kingdoms (such as Canada) as opposed to those (such as India) which are not.

Referendum A popular vote on a legislative proposal. Not used in the United Kingdom.

Reform Bill More accurately the Reform Act, 1832, which began the rationalization of representation in the House of Commons, and subsequent acts of a similar nature passed in 1867, and 1884.

Reformation The jurisdictional separation of the English and Scottish Churches from the Church of Rome and the reform of their doctrines and administration in the sixteenth century.

Regency (1) Commonly the period from 1810 to 1820 when the Prince Regent, later George IV, exercised the royal functions in the name of George III who was mentally ill.

(2) The right of certain princes (in a given statutory order) to exercise the royal functions while a reigning sovereign is under eighteen.

Registrar General The public official responsible for maintaining the central registers of births, marriages and deaths and for organizing and analysing the census.

Report Stage The stage in legislation where the conclusions of the Committee in the Committee Stage are reported to either House and an opportunity is given to the House as such to make further detailed amendments.

Restoration The return of Charles II to England in 1660.

Returning Officer (1) Any public officer who has to make a 'return', i.e. a formal reply to a writ.

(2) Especially a public officer responsible for conducting an election.

Right The body of political opinion which in general is satisfied with the existing position and opposes change or advocates change only at a slow pace.

Rump (1) The members of the House of Commons who remained after the various puritan purges of that body in the 17th Century.

(2) Generally any minority of a larger body claiming to exercise the power of the latter.

188

St James Palace The older of the royal residences in use in London. The official title of the British Court in diplomatic language is the 'Court of St James' and new sovereigns are still proclaimed there.

Sanction(s) This curious word has three divergent meanings:

(1) The agreement of a higher authority to something proposed to be done by a lower one.

(2) The means by which a high authority compels someone to do something he would not otherwise do.

(3) More recently the means short of violence by which it is sought through international action to control the activities of a State.

Second Reading The stage in legislation where the general principles of a bill are debated for the first time in either House of Parliament.

Secretary of State A high Minister, originally the Sovereign's Secretary.

Sederunt A Scottish term equivalent in minutes of 'present'. Originally used by the Courts of Session and Justiciary whose official minutes are called Books of Sederunt. These courts have long had certain powers of sublegislation (mostly procedural) which are accordingly called Acts of Sederunt.

Self Denying Ordinance Originally a measure passed by the puritan House of Commons requiring its members either to resign their military appointments or to resign from the House. Generally any measure aimed at preventing members of a legislature from holding paid government offices outside it.

Senate The Upper House of certain legislatures notably Northern Ireland and the United States of America.

Session (1) The period (between the Opening of Parliament and prorogation) within which all processes on a bill must be completed for it to become law.

(2) The period during which a law court functions.

Session, Court of The Supreme Civil Court of Scotland. The Outer House consists of a series of courts presided over by a single judge; the Inner House consists of several judges sitting as a court of appeal from the Outer House and from the Sheriff Courts.

Sheriff (1) In England an annually appointed officer who is now mainly responsible for enforcing court orders. Apart from the monarchy the office is the most ancient in the country.

(2) In Scotland a local judge.

Ship Money, Case of Charles I tried to levy this tax inland without the assent of Parliament. John Hampden refused to pay. He lost the case, but the arguments for the defence are the classic exposition of the doctrine that once the Crown has surrendered a right (in this case a right to tax) it cannot by itself resume the right.

Sinecure An office (paid or unpaid) without duties or functions. Mostly now abolished but a few are retained for special reasons of convenience, e.g. the Privy Seal to provide a non-specialist post in the Cabinet and the Chiltern Hundreds to make it possible for a member of parliament to resign.

Slavery Never lawful in England. Abolished in the colonies in 1833.

Slave Trade By British Subjects outside the United Kingdom, abolished 1807.

Solicitor A court officer who practises privately and who is responsible for managing the procedural side of litigation including the briefing of barristers.

Solicitor-General Now the Attorney General's deputy.

Somerset House The popular name for the central register of births, marriages, deaths and wills. It also contains the registry of the Probate Divorce and Admiralty Division of the High Court.

Sovereign (1) The reigning Monarch.

(2) The body invested with the legal power to make any law whatever. In the United Kingdom the Crown, Lords and Commons acting together in Parliament.

Speaker The chairman of a house in a legislature especially the chairman of the House of Commons at Westminster. He hardly ever speaks.

Speech from the Throne The Government's formal declaration of policy at the opening of a session of Parliament.

Standing Orders The rules governing the procedure of a debating assembly such as a council or House of Parliament. Those of the House of Commons are elaborate and detailed; those of the Lords much less so.

States The legislatures of Jersey and Guernsey.

Statute Act of Parliament or an order made under authority of such an Act.

Statutory Law That part of the law which has been made or enacted by a legislature.

Sublegislature An assembly capable of making laws, but subject to the overriding authority of a legislature.

Supplementary Estimate A request by the government to the House of Commons for more money than has been allowed for a particular head of expenditure in the previous budget.

Supplementary Question See Question Time.

Supremacy The statutory rule that the Sovereign is on earth supreme over the Church of England.

Supreme Court of Justice The highest court in England. (*See* Fig. 70.)

Surtax A tax supplementary to income tax levied upon persons with a comparatively high level of income.

Tallage A levy which medieval sovereigns occasionally made upon the tenants of royal estates. Long since regarded as illegal.

Tariff The amount or level of a customs duty.

Tax Any financial levy imposed by the central government.

Territorial Waters That part of the sea where the government of a country exercises sovereign powers. Until recently this was generally reckoned to be three miles from the coast, but oil and fishery disputes have led many countries to make much wider claims which are not necessarily admitted by other countries. In the case of Britain territorial waters extend for three miles.

In addition the British Government claims to control certain activities such as oil prospecting as far as the edge of the Continental Shelf in the Atlantic.

Third Reading The stage in legislation where a bill as amended in Committee and on Report is debated as a whole.

Thirty-Nine Articles The statement of fundamental doctrines held by the Church of England, and to which every ordained clergyman must formally assent.

Tithes An ancient income tax of 10 per cent charged on land for the benefit of the church. Commuted for redemption annuities which cease to be payable in 1996.

Toleration The withdrawal of legal disabilities from persons who are not members of the established church. Now complete.

Tory Conservative.

Treasury The central ministry which through its control of all revenues is the principal policy-making department.

The First Lord of the Treasury is the Prime Minister; the Chancellor of the Exchequer is the principal specialist minister and the chief government whips hold office as junior Lords.

Treaty An agreement or contract between nations, states or governments.

Trusteeship The modern name for the relationship between a former imperial power and one of its colonies. Membership of the United Nations involves an undertaking to prepare colonies for and eventually to grant them self government. This process is supervised by the United Nations Trusteeship Council, most of whose members have never had any colonies.

Tynwald The Manx Parliament.

Ulster Nowadays Northern Ireland, but anciently the present area of Northern Ireland plus the counties of Donegal, Monaghan and Cavan.

UNESCO United Nations Educational Scientific and Cultural Organization set up in 1946. Its most valuable function is to campaign against the substandard educational condition of underdeveloped countries.

Uniformity The statutory rule that the Church of England must use the Book of Common Prayer in its services. Nowadays often disobeyed.

Union Flag Commonly called the Union Jack, originally contained the English and Scottish crosses 1606; the Irish cross was added in 1801.

United Kingdom England, Wales, Scotland and Northern Ireland (but not the Channel Islands or Isle of Man).

UNO United Nations Organization set up under the United Nations Charter signed at San Francisco in 1945. General Assembly first met in London in 1945, since when the permanent H.Q. has been in New York. Its primary function is peace-keeping, but its subagencies are of growing importance in the field of health, education and food.

Ultra Vires Now the rule that a local authority cannot do anything involving expenditure of public funds unless specifically authorized by statute.

Verdict The finding of fact made by a jury.

Virement Parliament votes funds for particular purposes. Money not needed for one purpose may (subject to safeguards) be used for another. This switching of funds is called virement.

Wales Does not include Monmouth.

Westminster The normal seat of the British Parliament.

Westminster Palace Commonly known as 'The Houses of Parliament'. Originally a royal palace adapted for parliamentary use. Burnt down in 1834 and replaced by the present specially designed building. Damaged in World War II and partly reconstructed afterwards.

Westminster, Statute of The Act of 1931 which established the legal independence under the Crown of the original Dominions, i.e. Canada, Australia, New Zealand, South Africa, and Newfoundland. Of these South Africa is no longer in the Commonwealth and Newfoundland has become part of Canada. The Act forms the precedent for the creation of other independent countries.

Whigs The aristocratic political party formerly opposed to the Tories.

White Paper A document laid before Parliament by the government dealing with its detailed intentions on a particular issue of public importance.

Whitehall Now the street of ministries between Trafalgar Square and the Houses of Parliament. Sometimes used as synonymous with the government or the civil service.

Whitley Council A body representing teachers, the government and educational bodies which settles the pay and service conditions of teachers: also a similar body for other official employees.

W.H.O. World Health Organization. H.Q. Addis Ababa. A subagency of UNO concerned with exchange of medical information and combatting epidemics.

Witan (agemot) The ancient Saxon assembly of notables. The Kings council.

Windsor (1) A royal residence in the Thames Valley.
(2) The surname taken by the royal family in 1917.

Woolsack The seat from which the Lord Chancellor presides over the House of Lords. It is technically outside the House and can therefore be occupied by someone who is not a peer.

INDEX

Russia – *continued*
  Communist programme of aggression, 130–1
  changing impressions of, 142

St James's Palace, 189
Sanctions, diverse meanings of, 189
Scotland:
  established church (Presbyterian), 31
  Civil Law, 3, 21, 82
  local government, 3–4
  and the central government, 4
  Saxon borders, 6
  the Crown unified with England, 11
  Act of Union and, 12
  Secretary of State for, 54, 80
Second Reading, 189
Secretaries of State, 4, 51, 54, 189
  and by-laws, 80
  decline in prestige, 140
  their numbers and departments, 1868 and 1966, 173
Sederunt, explanation of, 189
Self Denying Ordinance, explanation of, 189
Senate, meaning of, 189
Session, meaning of, 189
  Court of, 189
Sessions, Parliamentary:
  extensions in 1966, 68, 114
  time available in, 114–15
  changes in procedure, 115–17
  introduction of morning sittings, 115–16
Sheriff, definition of, 189
Ship Money, Case of and implications, 189
Sinecure, definition of, 189
Slave Trade, 190
Slavery, 190
Social welfare:
  beginnings of government concern, 10
  industrialization and, 17
  ministries dealing with, 55
  voluntary organizations and, 109

Solicitor, definition of, 190
Solicitor-General, 190
Somerset House, 190
Sophia of Hanover, Electress, and the Crown, **46**
Sovereign, the:
  position in the Commonwealth, 4, 117, 128
  his advisers in Saxon times, 6–8
  and feudalism, 8
  financial resources in Middle Ages, 8–9
  the Stuarts and, 11, 12
  Bill of Rights and, 12
  resemblance to a party leader, 14
  symbol of national unity, 25
  means of support, 46–7
  and his legal powers, 47
  two absolute powers, 48
  the Privy Council and, 49
  speech from the Throne, 65
  assent to Bills, 69
  power to make Orders in Council, 79
  and the modern Prime Minister, 113
  Accession Proclamation, 159–60
Sovereignty:
  use of the term, 45
  component parts, 45
  changes in the central machine, 111, 113–14
  decline in its national aspect, 190
Space exploration, 140
Speaker, the:
  of the Lords, 62
  election of, 64
  and money Bills, 70
  and the Time Factor, 115
  his place in the House, 153, 190
Specialized organizations:
  influence on Government, 29–30
  membership of The 5000, 35
  local administration, 99–100
Speech from the Throne, 65, 190
Standing Orders, 190
Star Chamber, 10
'States, The', 4, 190